The Writer's Guide t

SELLING YOUR YOUR SCREENPLAY

The Writer's Guide to

SELLING YOUR SCREENPLAY

A top-selling Hollywood writer
tells you how to break into
the business—and stay there!

BY CYNTHIA WHITCOMB

The Writer Books

The Writer Books is an imprint of Kalmbach Trade Press, a division of Kalmbach Publishing Co. These books are distributed to the book trade by Watson-Guptill.

For all other inquiries, including individual orders or details on special quantity discounts for groups or conferences, contact:

Kalmbach Publishing Co.
21027 Crossroads Circle
Waukesha, WI 53187
(800) 533-6644

Visit our website at http://writermag.com
Secure online ordering available

Printed in Canada

02 03 04 05 06 07 08 09 10 11   10 9 8 7 6 5 4 3 2 1

Publisher's Cataloging-in-Publication

Whitcomb, Cynthia.
     The writer's guide to selling your screenplay : a top-selling Hollywood writer tells you how to break into the business—and stay there! / by Cynthia Whitcomb. — 1st ed.
     p. cm.
     Includes bibliographical references and index.
     ISBN 0-87116-192-3

     1. Motion picture authorship. 2. Television authorship—United States. 3. Motion pictures—Vocational guidance—United States. 4. Television—Vocational guidance—United States. I. Title.

PN1996.W362 2002   808.2'3
                          QBI02-200573

Art Director: Kristi Ludwig

This book is dedicated to my parents
David and Susanne Whitcomb
who told us from the cradle
we could be anything we wanted to be
and believed it.

Table of Contents

Preface

When I started out on the screenwriter's path, I looked for a book that would tell me everything I needed to know about the screenwriting business. I didn't find one and had to make a lot of my own mistakes. I've written this book with the hope you'll be able to avoid some of those.

I have been making my living as a screenwriter for over 20 years and have made more than $5 million writing. I have sold over 60 two-hour scripts, most of them for television movies to the three networks, and more than a dozen in feature development deals at major movie studios. Twenty-five of my scripts have been filmed and aired on prime-time network television.

I taught screenwriting at UCLA Film School for seven years. I've worked closely with hundreds of students, many of whom have gone on to successful screenwriting careers. Some have sold original screenplays for huge sums of money. And some have had a hard transition from the fantasy careers in their minds into the real world of the entertainment industry. This book exists to help them and you make that transition smoothly. By knowing what to expect and how to respond to success, as well as to rejection, I hope to save you some grief—to prevent you from burning out or giving up.

The prerequisites to this book are a degree of talent and a willingness to work hard. If you are prepared to write and rewrite until you get your screenplay into solid, polished, professional shape, then you are ready for this book.

My attitude was always, "I am smart and I am resourceful. Other people have done this who are basically no different from me. If they did it, I should be able to do it, too. Whatever I don't know, I can learn."

Maybe you've dashed off a script in a few weeks and you're sure you'll be independently wealthy by next month. You are going to be disappointed—not by me, but by a head-on collision with the realities of the business.

On the other hand, you may sell your first screenplay for a half million dollars or more. I've had students who've done it. But you need to be prepared for success even more than for failure. Being plunged suddenly into big-bucks, high-pressure, fast-lane Hollywood can be traumatic if you don't understand the rules of the game you're playing.

I hope this book will help you avoid those collisions of fantastic expectations with the way it really is. If you are a special, gifted new writer, I hope I can save you from crashing and burning in your first encounter with the industry. This is your survival manual.

Amateurs hope.
Professionals work.
—Garson Kanin

PART ONE

Breaking In

CHAPTER 1

My First Big Break

There are probably as many ways to break into Hollywood as there are people who've done it. You don't know which brick in the wall is going to give way and let you in, so you've got to keep knocking (pitching, punching, and pummeling) on all of them until one of them does. If you think you have to know somebody in Hollywood to break in, I am living proof that that's not the case. Here is my story.

I was not a child who grew up munching popcorn while watching Saturday matinees. I was almost 16 years old before I ever saw a movie. Both my grandfathers were Nazarene preachers, akin to Southern Baptists. Sins included drinking, dancing, smoking, and (cruelest by far) watching movies. A few months after *The Sound of Music* came out, a preacher friend of Dad's (bless his heart, wherever he is) mentioned that maybe this one movie might not be so sinful. So my dad packed up Mom and us four kids into the car, and we drove from Pasadena into Los Angeles to one of the huge old movie palaces on Wilshire Boulevard. We sat way up front because those were the cheapest seats.

Dad bought us popcorn, then the theater went dark. And the curtains opened and opened and opened, and suddenly we were soaring over the Austrian Alps in glorious Technicolor with music all around us. My jaw dropped about a foot. The popcorn was forgotten. I think I barely breathed for the next three hours. And my life was forever changed.

I learned two important things from this experience. First, that the church had lied to me about what was and was not sinful. Without further ado, I abandoned the stifling thinking of religious dogma, and broke out of adolescence ready to blossom with the sixties.

The second thing I learned was, "You don't have to be a nun." For this I will be eternally grateful to all involved, from the oldest, frailest nun to the littlest, most endearing Von Trapp munchkin.

By 17, a high school senior by day, I got a job selling popcorn at the Pasadena Esquire Theater in the evenings, sneaking in at every possible chance to watch stolen movie scenes. When *Gone With the Wind* came to the Esquire in one of its many revivals, I saw it so many times I could recite most of it by heart.

At 18, I was enrolled at UCLA Film School, watching all the classic films I had missed: Chaplin, Lubitsch, Sturges, Capra, Hitchcock, et al., making up for all those years of movies I had missed. I devoured them all, auditing extra classes beyond the maximum allowed, watching dozens of movies a week. One brilliant thing about a film school like UCLA is that the archives are stellar. A class in Hitchcock, for example, would include all of his films, in the order he made them, in their original near-perfect prints. It was a spectacular learning opportunity and I took full advantage of it.

I had known from early childhood that I wanted to be a writer. Now I knew what I wanted to write: Movies!

I started writing screenplays with a passion. Before I was even out of college I was writing as fast and as well as I possibly could. When I graduated, I moved back home and wrote like mad. I was afraid that if I took a full-time job, I wouldn't fulfill my dream. I'd take office temp jobs as a "Kelly Girl" for a few days at a time whenever I ran out of money. Many of the temp jobs wanted to keep me on as a regular employee, but I wasn't even tempted. I'd explain I was a writer, and a regular full-time job wouldn't leave me enough time to write.

In those first three years, I wrote ten full-length screenplays (three drafts each) before I ever sold anything. I tried a wide variety of genres and styles. Those ten scripts included a science-fiction brain-transplant script, a Disney-type family misadventure comedy, a western about the James brothers, a rock-band-on-the-road romp, a drug-running-in-Mexico downer, a wacky comedy about a dog catcher, a romantic comedy about a clown who drove a school bus, and a classic murder mystery set in 1930s Hollywood.

I sent all of these scripts out to 12 people each—mostly to people I didn't know, but knew of. Agents and producers. An occasional director or studio executive. These were names I had scrounged from anyone I knew who knew anyone. Names I had read in the paper. And all of them had passed.

But by the tenth script, I had learned to write screenplays by making most of the mistakes it's possible to make. All of which I'll try to help you avoid. The tenth was called *Grand Slam*, written in the style of *The Sting*. It was the story of a young ex-con, recently broken out of prison, trying to break into the newspaper business by uncovering the World Series fix of 1919. The story was exciting, well-structured, and had a fun, fast-paced style. I had read the *American Slang Dictionary* from cover to cover and incorporated every slang phrase that was used in Chicago circa 1919.

I sent *Grand Slam* out to a dozen places and still couldn't get to first base, so to speak. Everyone who read this script agreed that it was good work, but no one was offering to buy it or even represent it. I knew this was the best work I was capable of. I had been so sure that it would be the one to finally break through the brick wall for me that it was almost devastating to have it rejected, even with glowing praise, time after time. "It has problems. The protagonist is too young. There are no bankable 20-year-old stars. And the period is too expensive." In other words, no.

I knew I had to do something. Just then, a new movie came out, called *Hearts of the West*. It was an expensive film set in 1915 with a young protagonist played by Jeff Bridges. The script wasn't great. I felt mine was much better. I walked out of the theater frustrated and furious. "How come they made that picture and no one would make mine?"

Hearts was produced by Tony Bill, who had also produced *The Sting* (and won the Best Picture Oscar for it). I decided that if he liked both of them, he would have to love my script. I had read an article about him and his company in the *Los Angeles Times*, and he sounded like a young maverick who was looking for writers and making classy movies without being a big, inaccessible studio.

I called the Producers Guild of America and found out the address of his Venice, California, office. I was living in Long Beach at the time, so I gathered my courage and, script in hand, drove my little red '63 Volkswagen bug 45 minutes up the freeway to Venice and found his building. Unfortunately, when I got there it was lunchtime and no one was around. I finally tracked down a receptionist in a back room having lunch. She took my script and gave me a release form to sign. I had no cover letter, no acquaintances at the company, nothing to draw attention to the script except the words on the page. I drove home thinking, "What the hell . . . at least I tried."

Six days later, I woke up to find my VW had been stolen during the night. Of course, I had no insurance. No money. And now no car. Major bummer. This was 7:30 a.m. A few hours later, a little after 11 a.m. the phone rang and a voice said, "This is Tony Bill. I loved your script."

Finally, after three years of starving full time, writing my heart out, and a lifetime dream of being a writer, here was the moment when it was all suddenly paying off.

I suppose it doesn't always happen with one dramatic phone call, one single event that stands out so vividly in memory. But for me it did. I knew that those words coming over the wire were the beginning of another life. The opening line of a new career. And so it was. He asked me to come up and meet with him and talk about the script. We set a time. I hung up the phone and burst into tears. My first thought was, "God, if this is some kind of trade-off, keep the car."

I borrowed money from my parents to buy something I could wear to a meeting. I then had to borrow my Mom's Chevy Nova to drive up to it. But a couple of days later we met in his office. It was only *slightly* distracting that Tony was movie-star handsome like a young Warren Beatty. He said, "I loved your script. If I were going to shoot it, I wouldn't change a thing."

He then proceeded to tell me all the reasons why he *couldn't* shoot it. *Hearts* was not making money, there were no bankable stars who were right for it, and the period was too expensive. Did I know how hard it was to get cars from 1919? He owned a stable of cars from the 1930s. Could we set it in 1936? I would have loved to, but no one had fixed the World Series in 1936.

My heart was beginning to sink. Was this going to turn into another "you've-got-talent-kid-keep-trying" session? Then he said the magic words. "Let's do something else together." He gave me a novel he wanted adapted and said, "Read this. If you like it, maybe we'll do it." Now, think about this.

What do you think the odds are that I was going to come back and say I didn't like it? That's right. Zero to none.

I rushed home and devoured the book. You'd better believe that no matter what that book was, I would have come back with, "I love it and can make a movie out of it." I had been hungry too long.

The book was a novel, *Love Out of Season*, by Ella Leffland, wonderfully written but very bleak. The complete opposite of *Grand Slam*, it was a contemporary love story between an eccentric, reclusive woman artist and a shallow womanizer. An internal, psychological book about how these two people make each other miserable, until they finally break up and become even more miserable, it had no plot to play off. I was scared to death.

But I came back a few days later, trying to appear confident, as I said, "I think it can work. The first thing that needs to change is the guy can't be such a son of a bitch. He's completely unsympathetic . . ." And we went on from there.

At the end of the meeting, Tony said, "Let's do it. Who should I call to make your deal? Do you have an agent? I can suggest somebody if you don't."

I said, "That's okay. I know somebody. I'll call you tomorrow and give you his number." I was incredibly naive in many ways, but I knew enough intuitively not to take a producer's suggestion of an agent. Not that Tony was in any way trying to cheat me. It's just that, naturally, he'd prefer to negotiate a deal with a friend. You can't blame anyone for that. And if I hadn't known anyone to call, he would have been doing me a favor. Even the producer's friend is better than no agent at all.

But once you find yourself in this position, you obviously have a huge ace up your sleeve: someone wants to hire you.

Lee Rosenberg was a senior agent and partner of a prestigious, small literary agency, then called Adams, Ray & Rosenberg. He had been reading and rejecting my scripts and encouraging me for several years. He would always read them, and even return my calls, after only five or six days (compared to some agents who still haven't returned my calls). As always when I called his number, his assistant answered, saying he wasn't in and would I like to leave a message.

You bet I would. "Tell Lee that Tony Bill wants to hire me to write a feature and I'd like him to handle it, if he has the time." She took it down, and that very same day—about an hour later—Lee called me back with a casual, "What's up?" I explained the entire scenario to him and he said he'd be happy to negotiate the deal for me.

You probably realize without my telling you that there is scarcely an agent in town who wouldn't have agreed to make this deal. It was all set up; he just had to negotiate the terms and get 10% of my gross for making a few phone calls.

The next month was unbelievable hell to live through. It took them an entire month to make the deal. I was sure, on a daily basis, that it was going to fall apart and disappear. I was afraid Tony would change his mind and realize I was all wrong for the job. Or Lee would blow the deal. My list of demons was endless. But the deal finally was made. I would be paid Writers Guild minimum plus a bonus of six times that much if the picture got made. Not a bad deal. Certainly it was a fortune to me at the time.

I wrote the screenplay for Tony, doing several drafts, as is always done in development deals. When it was finished, he submitted it to MGM and they bought it outright in less than 48 hours. I didn't realize at the time that this was unusual, but I was pleased nonetheless. Now, the fact that MGM bought it meant nothing to me financially. Tony had paid me to write the screenplay and he owned it, so whatever he sold it for was his. But we were that much closer to making a movie.

Shari Lansing was our executive at MGM at the time, and she was excited and enthusiastic about the project. She thought it was "the best love story she'd read in a long time." There followed an amazing round of movie-star musical chairs. Ali MacGraw wanted to do it, but only with Nicholson. And Nicholson would only do it if Rafelson directed. And Rafelson was "somewhere in Mexico" shooting something else. Nolte might do it, but had another lady in mind. On and on it went, with never more than two of the three key pieces falling into place at the same time. It is still, many years later, on the shelf at MGM.

But what happened to me is what happens to many young writers whose first sold screenplay turns out well. The film wasn't made, but my reputation as a talented young screenwriter was. Word gets around. I turned in the final draft of *Love Out of Season* to Tony on a Friday. The following

Monday I started working on another screenplay for Twentieth Century Fox. Since then, I have sold an average of three screenplays a year.

The only thing that makes this story unique is that it happened to me. It is by no means an unusual example of what it's like to break into the screenwriting business. In many ways, it's a crapshoot. But even crap games have rules. And winners. But you have to know where the game is and whom to play with.

CHAPTER 2

Improving Your Writing Skills

A few years ago everyone with a college degree (and many without) had a novel in a desk drawer somewhere, or a secret ambition to write one. Times have changed that dream of writing a novel into the dream of writing a screenplay. Why is pretty obvious. A novel takes at least a year to write (sometimes several), a screenplay only a few months. If a novel is a bestseller, maybe a hundred thousand people will read it. If a movie is a hit, by the time it has gone from screen to foreign release to television to DVD, hundreds of millions of people may well have seen it. Finally, an average first novel, if it sells at all, might bring $7,000 to its overworked author. Most screenplays written on spec that do sell make at least $100,000. Sometimes they go for ten times that amount.

But you can't just change your software to screenplay format. Screenwriting is a highly specialized process. There are structural necessities, a rigid format, stylistic peculiarities, and many other writing demands particular to the form. It is important to learn the basics of three-act structure and how to format a script. If it is not written in the right format, people will flip through it, decide at a glance that it was written by an amateur, and toss it. You must learn the basics if you hope to compete with the rest of the scripts coming in.

How do you learn to write screenplays?

Reading

Today most bookstores have sections on screenwriting. (See reading list in Appendix D.) Many of the books are good. My favorite, of course, is *The Writer's Guide to Writing Your Screenplay* (The Writer Books, 2002), which was written by an author you are already familiar with, me. In addition to teaching solid three-act structure and screenplay format, it takes a global approach to the process, which breaks down into four equally important elements: The Spine, The Heart, The Mind, and The Spirit.

It is also extremely helpful to read screenplays. *Scenario* magazine publishes three complete screenplays in every quarterly issue. Many screenplays are also published in paperback book form. But the most practical way to access screenplays is to download them off the internet. Many are free. Some cost a nominal fee to download. (See Appendix C.)

Studying Movies

Your local video store can be a low-budget, do-it-yourself film school. You can teach yourself a great deal about writing screenplays by watching movies carefully. But you can't learn much from terrible movies. If everything in the script was done wrong, it won't have much to teach you. Instead, study the masters.

If you want to write suspense, create your own Hitchcock symposium. Rent and watch his greatest movies until you get the style, pacing, tone, structure, all of it. Pick your favorite movie in the style you are aspiring to work in and then study all of the films by that screenwriter or director. Get a stopwatch and begin to measure how long those scenes last. It seems like a couple of minutes. Is it actually only 48 seconds? You need to teach yourself how to gauge scene lengths. One minute of screen time is equivalent to one page of screenplay.

If I want to sharpen my suspense, I'll do a Michael Mann week. Update my style? I'll get into Guy Ritchie. Tighten my romantic comedy dialogue? Richard Curtis marathon coming right up. Fast-paced, dramatic dialogue? *A Few Good Men* gets shoved into the VCR and the volume pumped up. Even after years of writing screenplays for a living, I still do this regularly. There is always more to learn, and great new movies are being made all the time.

You can develop your screenwriting skills by "doctoring" movies you see. Watch a movie two or three times and take it apart. Begin with "What's wrong with this movie? What didn't work?" Then go directly to: "How would I fix it? How could it have been better? What would I have changed?"

If you're committed to learning everything you can, studying movies can be a goldmine.

Writers' Groups

These regular gatherings can be a great tool, whether organized by a club or college or just an informal gathering of friends who are also writers.

When I was starting out, I belonged to a group of seven young writers who met every Wednesday night to take turns reading our work out loud. We'd make comments and brainstorm together.

There are several benefits to this type of support group.

1 Hear your script out loud. This is the best way to find out if the pacing is working. And if the dialogue is good. Your ear has heard thousands of hours of movie dialogue. But your eye has only read a fraction as many screenplays. Trust your ear. If the writers in your group are not accomplished actors, this is best. A good line will work, even if not read brilliantly. And a bad one can be helped too much by a gifted actor. It is always better to recognize the bad lines and fix them as early as possible.

2 Have an imposed deadline. If you have to come up with a script to read or a new, greatly revised draft of a script to read every seven weeks as I did, you'll get a lot more written than if you are writing with no outside reinforcement. No one wants to be the one to show up with his tail between his legs, with nothing for the group to work on that week. Deadlines are godsends.

3 Find out if your funny lines are actually funny. It can be embarrassing to find out that your jokes aren't funny. But it is extremely difficult to tell what is actually funny struggling alone in a room. Knowing where the laughs really are can be enormously helpful, whether your script is a comedy or just has a few funny moments, which all scripts should have.

4 Get feedback from your fellow writers. I have listed this fourth for a reason. It can be a great gift, but it can also be a problem. Please keep in mind that another person's opinion is only an opinion. He or she will not always be right. Use the note only if it makes sense to you. Never try to fix something if you don't understand how it is broken. Or how the suggestion makes it better. Do not revise sideways. In other words, don't make it different if you don't get how the suggested change makes it better. And for heavens sake, don't use a suggestion that you feel makes it worse, just because the others all agree that it should be another way. It is your baby. Your vision. Your movie. Protect it.

5 Boost your morale. It gets lonely sitting for hours in a room with only the products of your own imagination. Especially if you have the bad luck (as I have) of being a writer by trade and an extrovert by nature. Having people you can talk with about your work can be the thing that saves you from giving up on the whole lonely enterprise. You're not alone. There are many, many just like you in rooms all over America. Make the effort to connect. The comradeship can really help you get through the week. It can also be invaluable to have somebody in the group you can call in between meetings and say, "Remember that scene in the train yard? If it starts with them finding a dead dog on the tracks, does that help me? Am I crazy?"

It's also wonderful to be able to rush back to your group to celebrate when you sell your first script, sign with your first agent, or get your first big check. As Mark Twain so aptly put it, "a grief can be endured alone, but a joy wants company." If you make the Nicholl quarterfinals, you need people who know what that means ready to break out the champagne.

The group I belonged to met every week for several years. Five of us went on to careers in writing. The other two found careers in professional stage management and creating special effects for movies. So what we learned as a group about writing and dramatic structure benefited us all.

There was a famous screenwriters' group awhile back with an apartment in Hollywood known as the "Pad O'Guys" or POG. As the name implies, they were all young males and they sold several screenplays, most notably *Lethal Weapon*. They were the screenwriters equivalent of the Brat Pack, though they sometimes referred to themselves as "the Algonquin Round Table of the eighties." Would it have been successful if it were merely one Pad O'Guy? Maybe, but the victory party would have tanked.

It is not too difficult to find others like yourself who are serious about screenwriting and to start your own circle. All it takes is a room, a pot of coffee, and the eagerness to write as well as you possibly can.

Film Schools

Four film schools used to dominate the field: UCLA, USC, NYU, and Columbia. But today most colleges and universities have film departments and courses in screenwriting. You don't have to go to any special film school to learn screenwriting. Nor is a degree from a prestigious film school likely to do much for a screenwriter's career. Film schools or degrees in film are not necessary; they are a luxury. If you can pursue that route, by all means go for it. Ideally, film school is a protected space where you can devote all of your time and energy to pursuing this one goal: becoming a screenwriter.

The other advantage to a really high-caliber film school is the access to great archives, as I mentioned in the last chapter. But more and more, classic films are available on tape and DVD.

To launch a successful screenwriting career, the only essential requirement is a great script. In order to write a great script, you have to master the form. This can be done by taking screenwriting classes, joining writing groups, reading screenplays and screenwriting books, renting movies and studying them at home, or—my own choice—all of the above. And most important, by writing a lot of scripts. Stephen King said it well in his book *On Writing:* "If you want to be a writer, you must do two things above all others: read a lot and write a lot." Amen. And to that I would add, for screenwriters, "See a lot of movies."

CHAPTER 3

The Calling Card Script

It is finally written! You've reached that goal, typed a page number with three digits in it and written in caps at the end of the scene those blessed words FADE OUT. What do you do with it now?

The first script you complete, the one ready to be sent out into the world and good enough to represent you as a writer, will be your "calling card" script. I know you are hoping and praying that someone will fall in love with it and send you a check for a million dollars. While this does happen occasionally, it's more likely—if the script is good enough—that people who read it will be interested in you as a writer and may want to hire you to write a different script for them. This is why it's your "calling card."

Don't Send It Out Too Quickly

I know how strong the urge will be for you to put it straight into the mail. The creative process has a natural high attached to it, which you doubtless already know if you've written your first script. The thrill of accomplishment and the amazed feeling of "where did it all come from" can make the script seem perfectly wonderful in that glow of the moment.

At this point writers often make a mad dash to send it off. Only later do they reread it, after it's cooled off a little, and find holes in the plot, things they forgot to set up, typos, and all kinds of little things that could have been better.

If you send out your screenplay half-baked, people will read it and think, "Not great," and pass. I know you're thinking, "So what? I'll send it back to them when it's great and they'll be impressed with how much better it is and they'll love it." Wrong. They won't read it again.

Producers, executives, and agents have stacks of scripts coming to them. If by chance they do pick up your revised script and don't remember your name or the title, they'll read one or two pages and then realize they've read it before. It'll get tossed aside once more, even though it may be a great script now.

A producer friend of mine discovered a very talented, unproduced new writer who had a screenplay with a terrific story. *"Rear Window* meets *Stand by Me"* was the pitch line. The producer was very excited about the script, but it was a first draft and needed polishing. She showed it to an agent who felt the same way. They encouraged the writer to polish the script, but he refused. The writer wanted them to sell it for him—as is—and then he would be willing to rewrite it for a large sum of money.

So they sent the script to a prominent executive producer with a studio deal and he loved it, too. Now the script had an agent, a producer, and an executive producer; it was a story that everyone was tremendously excited about by a talented writer with a unique voice. It was then submitted to nearly all the major studios with big-name directors, most of whom considered it seriously for a week or two. Several times it came close to selling. But the final decision was negative. The script just wasn't *quite* strong enough to top the scales. And so they all passed. No sale.

This story could easily have been different. Whether because of laziness or arrogance or simply naïve impatience, the writer didn't finish his job. A script only has one shot at a sales campaign like this. And this script failed. The writer finally went back and rewrote the script, but it was too late. His script had already been "hot" and made the rounds. There was little chance that it would be hot again. It had been covered by all the majors and those doors were closed.

Hollywood really is a small town. People will talk about you. Oh, yes. Anonymous you. Your name and your work will get around. You don't want to be known for sloppy work. Conversations like this are common:

FIRST D.P. (Development Person): I just got a teenage vampire script in, which is what Bob is looking for, but it's a writer I've never heard of. Jonathan Doe.

SECOND D.P.: Oh, yeah. I read that. We passed.

Now the first D.P. can save himself an hour or two. He can pass on your script without even reading it.

But don't be discouraged by the movie community's love of gossip. Later on it could well work in your favor. It's one of the ways people get "hot."

Yours can't be just another okay script. Or even another pretty good script. Many new writers watch a mediocre movie and think, "Hey, I could write better than that." Simply writing better than something lukewarm is not going to make it. If someone picks up a script that is like the rest of the junk you see every day, why should they buy it? Obviously they've already got it.

In order for a script to sell it has to be good enough to generate great enthusiasm with several levels of executives.

The point is you can't afford to do anything less than your absolutely best work. Which almost always means several drafts.

How to Get Feedback

Getting feedback is an important step to find the clarity and insight you need for that essential rewrite. It will make your script better and sharper. Seeing your script through another's eyes can remind you of things that were in your mind, but somehow didn't make it onto the page. It can give you a clearer vision so that scenes to which you had become blind are newly illuminated. Now, they can be polished and honed with objectivity.

On the downside, it can also be depressing and sometimes even devastating. In my early twenties, I once spent a year writing a novel that a close friend, another writer, spent two hours criticizing, culminating with his advice that I throw it out. "Chalk it up to experience. To learning to write." I didn't follow his advice and instead did some minor rewriting. The book went on to win third place in the Samuel Goldwyn Writing Award, with (to me at the time) a considerable cash award attached. Winning third place in this contest also opened agents' doors.

Choose your critics carefully. Your first instinct may be to give it to your mother, spouse, roommate, or best friend. While some of these people may be bright, literate, and articulate, they may also tend either to love everything you do, or to be overly critical. Your best bet would be another writer with whom you can trade scripts and who would most likely appreciate the need for tough but tactful, constructive criticism. Try to find someone who shares your taste in movies. A Tarantino fan may not be very helpful to your romantic comedy script.

A note of precaution: You both must understand that ideas offered as feedback are given freely. If they become part of the script, they belong to the scriptwriter. The unwritten agreement is that you will do the same for their scripts in return.

These questions to be asked of the reader may be helpful in getting the most constructive feedback:

- Where did you lose interest?
- Was the plot clear? Anything you didn't understand?
- Did you like characters A, B, C? (You need to know if readers like the characters that are meant to be sympathetic. If not, pinpoint the moment at which they were turned off by dialogue or actions.)
- Were you ahead of the story? When?
- Was there anything I repeated too much or was too heavyhanded about?
- Did you laugh? Where?
- Were you moved? By what?
- Did you guess the ending?
- Was it a page turner or did you put it down a lot?
- Was it believable? What didn't you believe?

"The Dirty Dozen"

Producer/Director Tony Bill has probably discovered more new writers that became huge than any other person in Hollywood. Among them are Terrence Malick (*The Thin Red Line*), David S. Ward (*Sleepless in Seattle*), Paul Schrader (*Taxi Driver*), Curtis Hanson (*L.A. Confidential*), John Patrick Shanley (*Moonstruck*), and many, many more, including myself.

Tony has put together a list for new writers of the 12 Things Not to Do before sending a script out. "There is no excuse for a script handed in that does not meet these simple, precise, technical, kindergarten-level require- ments." He has generously allowed me to elaborate on his "Dirty Dozen" to ensure a higher quality of screenplays arriving in Hollywood. You probably know most of these already, but any one of them could make the difference between a script sold or scrapped.

Tony Bill's Dirty Dozen

1 Don't use a fancy cover. The simpler the better. No artwork, hand lettering, photos, or gimmicks. Make sure it is soft-bound cardstock or flexible plastic, not a hardcover notebook. (A producer has to be able to roll it over and hold it in one hand to read while sipping that margarita or smoking that big cigar by his pool.) The script should be on three-hole-punched white paper (20-pound, standard typing paper) bound with three heavy brads of adequate weight to hold it together when one gets halfway through, or "script screws" if you can find them. (Script screws or the heavy 1¼" brads can be ordered from The Writers Store in L.A. (310) 441-5151. http://www.writersstore.com) You can neatly print the title along the bound edge with a fine-tipped black felt pen, if you like.

2 Don't include a list of characters or their biographies. The script has to stand on its own and the characters have to be introduced well, so it's clear who they are, how they're related, and whether or not they're the leads.

3 Don't suggest casting. It has become common practice in a pitch to mention that "Courtney" could be played by Julia Roberts or Sandra Bullock, but don't ever mention an actor's name in a screenplay. (More on this in Chapter 4.)

4 The title page should be as simple as possible. Centered: The Title. Beneath it: An Original Screenplay by Your Name. At the bottom right: Contact information, whether it is an agent's name, address, and phone number or yours. Don't ever date a script unless it's already sold. (You would be shocked at how fast something gets "old" in Hollywood.) Don't ever number a draft. (They'll be insulted that you've bothered to send them a "First Draft" and critical that it's only this good for a "Fourth Draft.") It's a no-win phrase; don't include it. Once a script has sold and you're being paid to rewrite it, the dates and draft numbers function as invoices (i.e., "I delivered the third draft on 3/25. Please pay me."). Tony feels that you should not write "Registered WGA" on the cover page. If you want to include it, write it small at the bottom of the back side of the title page. You should definitely register it with the WGA. Just don't advertise it too boldly. The number of script thefts in the industry is tiny. And paranoia almost always signifies an amateur.

5 Don't include a synopsis. It encourages producers not to read your script. If they want it covered, they can have their own people cover it. Then later if they don't buy it, you can chat up an assistant over the phone and possibly get a copy of your coverage, thereby gaining valuable insight into why it didn't sell and what it needs in order to do so.

6 Do not apologize in a cover letter. Not for *anything* in the script, from misspelling to plot holes. If it's not as good as it can possibly be, don't send it. Fix it. An apologetic cover letter will send your script straight into the shredder.

7 Don't include camera angles or other technical directions. That's the director's job and it irritates them to have you tell them how to shoot a picture. Never use CLOSE SHOT, PAN, ZOOM IN, ANGLE ON, DISSOLVE TO, TWO SHOT or any of the dozens of others you happen to know. The one exception is on the rare occasion when it is absolutely necessary for a story point. For example, if two people are having a midnight supper in their hotel suite, and at a precise point in the dialogue you want ANGLE TO INCLUDE the man standing behind the window curtain watching them— okay. In that case, spell it out. Otherwise let the director do his job.

8 Don't suggest actor's readings parenthetically. (See Chapter 4 for more detail on this.)

9 It has to be the right length. Don't submit a screenplay less than 100 pages or more than 135 pages long. And don't cheat by using wide margins or changing font size. Screenplays are printed in Courier or Courier New fonts, size 12. The pages should have 1″ margins on the top, right, and bottom. The 1½″ to 2″ margins on the left will accommodate three-hole-punched paper. The average film script runs 110 to 120 pages, which translates into a minute of film per page of script.

10 Don't leave a word misspelled. With spell-check programs on most computers it is easier to produce perfect clean scripts. But you still have to read carefully, every word. I once read to the climactic scene of a student's action screenplay and in the heat of battle, instead of "squeezing off a shot" the poor hero had a hilariously mis-typed vowel in that important noun. I know producers who will pass on a script if it has half a dozen typos or mistakes in the first ten pages. If the writer doesn't care enough to make it clean, they don't waste their time.

A short note here on the most commonly misspelled words by screenwriters that spell-check software won't find. Lightning does not have an "e" in it. Lightening is also a word, but it is not a noun and it's not what you mean. Metal, medal, and meddle are all words but they are not interchangeable. Make sure you're using the one you need. Likewise pedal, petal, and peddle.

11 Don't number scenes. Scene numbers are only for shooting scripts, not selling scripts. They are for breaking down scripts for location and budget purposes and to schedule the shoot. It's wonderful that you've bought fancy software, but shut off the scene-numbering function.

12 Use a good-quality printer or high-quality copier. Laser printing or its equivalent. If it's not crisp, clear, and clean, it's canned.

Register Your Script

When it is ready, before you send out a single copy to anyone in the Industry, register your screenplay with the Writers Guild of America. You don't have to be a member. It costs $20 to register a script, and they will keep a copy of your script on file for five years. After that, you can renew the registration if you haven't yet sold it. Once your script is registered with the WGA, if someone should plagiarize your work, you can prove that you had the script at the date of registration.

You can register by mail or go online for the most current information. Writers Guild of America 7000 W. Third St., Los Angeles, CA 90048. Telephone: (323) 782-4700. Web site: www.wga.org.

The Second Script

Now that your first screenplay is out there making the rounds, you should be ready to write a second (or third, fourth, or fifth). This next script should be different from the first in setting, genre, or character. You want to demonstrate a range of your abilities with sample screenplays that contain a variety of subject and style.

As I said in Chapter 1, the first screenplay that got me work was a period adventure comedy in the style of *The Sting*. My next was a psychological drama and love story—contemporary, urban, internal, and dark. On reading these two strong samples, people assumed I could probably write anything in between. As a result I got a lot of work from these two scripts alone.

At least one of your first screenplays must be contemporary if you want to get work. Most of the features made today are set in the present. That's where the market is.

If you are wed to a genre, then you can ignore the advice in the last couple of paragraphs. If you're a comedy writer, for example, and that's all you do and all you want to do, then God bless you. Go for it. If you can make people laugh out loud reading words on the page, you ought to be independently wealthy in short order. But even in writing your next comedy script, you should stretch the envelope as much as you can. Even if it's only a shift from high-school sex comedy to frat-house sex comedy. John Hughes, practically the father of teen wish-fulfillment hits, alternated between fulfilling adolescent girls' fantasies *(Sixteen Candles, Pretty in Pink)* and teen boy dreams *(Weird Science, Ferris Bueller's Day Off)*. Find a range for yourself and play every note.

So you're ready to roll. Your script has had feedback and has been polished, proofread, corrected, and copied. It's neatly planted between flexible covers and has been registered with the WGA. Now it's ready to fly.

CHAPTER 4

What Hollywood Is Looking For

It is futile to try to anticipate what Hollywood is looking for on a week-to-week basis. The lead time on feature films is more than a year. Even if you subscribe to the daily trade papers and try to stay on top of every project at every studio, by the time a movie hits big with a gigantic opening weekend, you can't throw a similar script together fast enough to compete with the studios' own stockpiles of scripts. They already have ten more kung fu scripts on hand ready to go if one hits. You can't win this game. It is not a business where jumping on the latest fads works for newcomers.

What does work is to be well versed in what Hollywood is always looking for year in and year out. To find out what that is, I interviewed several dozen insiders: producers, agents, studio executives, and directors. Because so many of their answers covered the same ground, I have simplified their answers into a definitive list of what Hollywood is looking for in a screenplay.

Is It Castable?

The reality of the movie business today is that if you want to give your script the best chance of selling to Hollywood, it needs to be castable. If the producers/agents/executives can't easily imagine that a star will want to act in your story, then it will probably never be bought, let alone made.

According to John Willis's *Screen World 2000*, the current list of the top ten box office stars is (in order, few surprises here): 1. Julia Roberts, 2. Tom Hanks, 3. Adam Sandler, 4. Bruce Willis, 5. Mike Myers, 6. Tom Cruise, 7. Will Smith, 8. Mel Gibson, 9. Meg Ryan, 10. Sandra Bullock. I am making up numbers 11 to 20, but here are my educated guesses in no particular order: Russell Crowe, Harrison Ford, Jim Carrey, Robin Williams, Brad

Pitt, George Clooney, Nicolas Cage, Michael Douglas, Michelle Pfeiffer, and Ben Affleck. This list will change slightly each month, of course, as new movies hit big. And by the time this book goes to press some of the young guns may have broken through to stardom: Jude Law, Hugh Jackman, Heath Ledger, Josh Hartnett, and the like. You get the idea. Think in terms of stars like these.

If you have written a protagonist or villain that would interest an actor of this caliber, you're halfway home. If not, review this brief checklist to help you get there and head back to your computer for a rewrite.

• Think 3-D. Give the character more than one dimension. Internal conflict.

• Don't be too specific about physical description. Don't say exactly how old, tall, etc. If you describe the protagonist as six foot two, blond hair, and blue eyes, how many stars in the top 20 box office draws fit that description? None

• Don't be specific about the character's age unless he/she is under 18.

• Don't mention any actor's name such as "a Harrison Ford type."

• Give the main character a big entrance. A first moment. A great description. Actors decide fast if the part is good enough.

• Give the lead the good lines. Don't give all the best laughs to the comic sidekick.

• Don't make the main character stupid, unless you're doing *Rainman*. He needs to be ahead of the audience.

• Don't tell an actor how to act with parenthetical directions (angrily), etc.

• Include an "Oscar Clip-worthy" scene.

Ultimately the most important thing you can do is to fall in love with the character yourself. If it's someone you love, chances are an actor will catch that, like a highly contagious, wonderful virus that will infect a star with that same passion.

Is It Fresh, Original, Surprising?

Does it have an original premise like *Memento, Sliding Doors,* or *Run Lola Run?*

Does it have an original style like *Snatch* or *Oh Brother, Where Art Thou?*

Does it have original twists of storyline? Do set-ups we've seen before have completely different payoffs than we expect, like *Pulp Fiction* or *Fargo?*

Is the dialogue fresh and cliché-free? Do the characters say things that surprise and delight?

What Are They Looking For in a Script?

Great story with a hook, a beginning, middle, and end.

A thumping good story. A great yarn.

A script that's alive. "It feels real. It's completely believable."

An original voice. Surprising, offbeat, different.

Dialogue that is non-expository. Real voices speaking.

Quality and taste.

A hero's evolution. Transformation of character. Growth.

Characters who behave in original but believable ways.

Is it commercial? Can it be pitched in a sentence or two?

Are there unique moments that we haven't seen before?

Is there legitimate emotion? Do we care?

Is it about something? An issue? A theme?

What Are They Looking For in a Screenwriter?

Passion. Someone who is more visual than verbal. Humor.

Someone I can work with, who is not intractable.

Flexibility.

Style.

Intelligence.

Continuous inventiveness.

Someone who can get unstuck and keep coming up with new ideas.

Someone who is good company.

What Turns Them Off?

Easy solutions. Writing that is too on the nose.

Gratuitous violence.

Shallowness. Flash over substance.

Recycling old movies instead of coming up with new ones.

The Bottom Line

If your screenplay meets the criteria above, it still needs to succeed in bringing it all together.

It boils down to this. Your screenplay has to make them do two things: *Care.* And *believe.*

If you can be objective enough to pretend you are sitting on the other side of the desk, reading a new script, and what you see makes you care and believe, then your script is ready to send out. If not, keep revising until your characters are interesting, your storyline is fresh, and you have a script that comes alive.

CHAPTER 5

Sending It Out

For this stage of your career to really take off, you should organize your efforts with as much care and concentrated energy as if you were planning and executing a political or military campaign. Keep careful track of what you send, to whom, and when, so when you get a response, you won't be fumbling around trying to remember which company he's with or which script he's calling about. This will also make following up much simpler. You'll be able to say with certainty, "I sent Mr. Lucas a copy of my script *Star Truckers* on July 17 and I'm calling to see if he's had a chance to read it yet."

Where Do I Send My Script?

To whom should you send it first? Agents? Producers? Actors? Your script is hot off the press and as clean and lean as you can make it. I suggest you begin with:

Screenwriting Contests

Having won or placed in a screenwriting competition can get the attention of studios and agents faster than an unknown name can. Here are three examples I know personally:

Me. As I mentioned in Chapter 3, even winning third place in the Samuel Goldwyn Writing Award competition at UCLA made agents willing to read my work. And I didn't even win for a screenplay. I could say in a query letter, "I was one of the winners of the Samuel Goldwyn Award last year (notice I didn't say third place) and would love for you to read my screenplay." Okay, I kind of make it sound like I won for a screenplay, but I didn't lie about it. It didn't launch my career, but it did put me in a position to know and call an agent to make my first deal once I got a toe in the door.

Mike Rich. Mike is a local boy up here in Oregon, a familiar morning radio voice on KINK-FM, who wrote a good script. He got an agent to send it around Hollywood. But no nibbles. Everybody passed. Entered it in the Nicholl Fellowship and it won. An auction followed. The script sold to one of the studios that had already passed on it, and for seven figures with a second script deal thrown in as a sweetener. That script was *Finding Forrester* and the second was the Disney/Dennis Quaid movie *The Rookie*.

Max Adams. Living in Utah, she won both Austin and the Nicholl. Her spec script *Excess Baggage* was produced and starred Alicia Silverstone and Benecio Del Toro. By the time she arrived in Hollywood she was the hottest thing in town.

So I encourage you to enter screenwriting contests. You are gathering assets to use in query letters, as crowbars to help you pry open the golden gates of the studios. A list of the top screenwriting contests is included in Appendix E.

The List

Who do you know? The old saying that in Hollywood it all depends on who you know is not entirely true. But it *can* help if you do know someone somewhere in the industry, who can get someone to read your script.

Don't panic. You can't have fewer contacts than I did when I wrote my first script. As I told you, I came from a large family of preachers and teachers who believed movies were sinful. Get out a piece of paper and start listing people you know who are either in the entertainment industry, or are related to or know someone who is. Think. I know that you know someone. Even if you live in Iowa.

I once wrote a letter to a prominent director that said, "Dear Mr. X, My friend Sheldon's father knew you at Cornell University twenty years ago. Would you please read my screenplay?" He actually did read it and was willing to sit down over coffee and offer constructive advice.

Do you have a list now? Think hard. Be creative. Be willing to take some risks here. At this point, don't worry if it's ten names, three names, or none. We're just beginning. I'll give you some ideas.

Agents

The Writers Guild website (www.wga.org) has a free, up-to-date, down-loadable, list of screenwriters' agents. There are also books that catalog screenwriters' agents. These generally have more information on each agent, but don't include as many.

How do you narrow the list to the most likely prospects? You could, of course, blanket the field, since multiple submissions are acceptable in Hollywood. But one shortcut for finding the best agent for your type of script is to read movie credits and make note of the writers who are writing the movies you love. Then call the Writers Guild, Agency Department, at (323) 782-4502 or check online (www.wga.org) and find out who represents the writer. They'll give you the specific agent's name and the agency. Then you can write a letter that says, "I really admire the way you have handled Mr. Goldman's career . . ."

Directors, Producers, and Stars

If there is a director you consider the best choice on the planet to do your screenplay, someone you have admired for years, or a producer who does all the best movies in your particular genre, by all means let them know how you feel about them and send them your screenplay. They are remarkably easy to find.

Simply call the Producers Guild of America (323) 960-2590 and ask for the producer's address and phone number. Don't be shy or intimidated. It's their job to put you in touch with someone who represents him, or someone through whom you can reach the producer. The Directors Guild number is (310) 289-2000.

Most actors are not the kind of people who make movies happen. They are more likely to be the kind of people that field offers. They read scripts that have offers attached. In other words, most of them are not producers. But some stars have their own companies and actually produce movies. When you start looking into this, you'll start to get a feel for which stars find scripts and which ones field them.

Barbara Streisand, for example, is a real producer and director. So are Jodie Foster, Tom Hanks, and several others. Some of them are occasional producers. Look into the ones that are right for your project. If you call the

Screen Actors Guild (323) 954-1600, they will give you the name and address of the star's production company or who manages him or her. You can query Mel Gibson with the same stamp and envelope you'd query an agent with. Why not? They are all long shots at this point. Take them all.

Query Letters

Send query letters to agents and producers. Make sure your letters are enthusiastic, sincere, and original. Be fearless and bold. It's their business to find talented screenwriters. They are looking for *you*.

The query letter should be well written, bright, original, and have a hook in it. Tell them a little bit about yourself, what you have written, and briefly about the script you want to send them. The one sentence pitch. Enough to make them want more. Don't send the script unless they request it.

Some of you, I know, hesitate to give away your unique idea in a cover letter for fear of it being stolen. But agents are not in the business of developing scripts, so it is unlikely they will steal an idea. Besides, if they did something like that, writers would report them to the Guild and they'd soon be off the list. And it would be faster and cheaper for a producer to buy your script than to have someone else rip off your idea.

They are looking for writers with good scripts. And the only way to get them to read you is to put the great story of your terrific, polished script into the letter. I strongly recommend that you take this leap of faith. If you spent two weeks working on this one-page query letter, it would be time well spent. It may be the most important single page you ever write.

The Hook (How to Get Their Attention)

The hook in your query letter might be that you have won a screenwriting contest, as I mentioned above. An agent will be much more likely to ask to read a script that has already beaten a field of contenders and won a writing award, *any* writing award.

Or the hook might be that your script is something you are uniquely qualified to write. If you can truthfully say, for example, "I have an action adventure script based on my own experience in the Navy Seals," go for it. This kind of statement in a cover letter will definitely grab their attention. One of my students was actually a brain surgeon who took a year off to try screenwriting. He, of course, mentioned this in his query letter describing his suspense thriller about a senator who is sabotaged during neurosurgery. The agent not only requested that script, he sold it.

If the query letter is funny, this can also be a hook. If it has a couple of real laughs in a single page of the query letter, they will probably want to read your whole screenplay.

Be sure to always address your query to a *person* at an agency or studio, not just to the name of the company. If something is sent to "ICM," it will go directly from the mailroom into the recycling bin.

A Sample Query Letter

Dear Mr. Spielberg,

Having loved movies like *Home Alone* and your *Indiana Jones* trilogy when I was a kid, I wanted to write a movie I could take my kids to that they'd remember like that years from now.

e-tickets is that movie.

When their Dad disappears and the media accuses him of stealing a hundred million dollars from his company, Jake, Jordy, and their half-sister Lizzy decide to save Dad. Their wild adventure takes them around the world in six days. Through the catacombs under the city of Paris, where in addition to millions of skeletons, they find the French crown jewels stolen in 1789. A high-speed car chase with 16-year-old Lizzy driving a Ferrari across France, a rescue by Hummer from a near-kidnapping in the marketplace in Cairo, and 12-year-old Jake flying a stolen Navy fighter jet off the deck of an aircraft carrier in the Indian Ocean.

They are pursued by Cole Hunter, an adventurer/mercenary who funds his solo assaults on K2 by being the world's highest-paid bounty hunter. He chases the kids around the world, in pursuit of their father, with orders not to bring him back alive.

My kids are lucky to live in a time when special effects make it possible to film anything we can imagine.

Imagine *e-tickets*.

You can query by regular letter or by e-mail. I would not query by fax. Send your query letter to as many agents as you like. I don't recommend "cold calling" agents unless you have some kind of in (know someone, etc.). But follow-up calls after they've requested a script are fine.

You have to get his interest. If he were only planning to stop and pay attention to one unknown this year, why would he choose *you*? Convince him that you have the very thing he is looking for.

Pitch-a-thons and Writers' Conferences

These are also a way to find agents. Pitch-a-thons are relatively new; however, it costs quite a bit to spend two minutes pitching to agents and producers who are bombarded with hours of two-minute pitches. It is unlikely they will remember yours. And most stories take longer than two minutes to pitch well. I've heard that one of the big Hollywood pitch-a-thons, while drawing hundreds of writers per year, has only resulted in a total of four deals in the last six years. So the odds are not great. But if it is convenient and sounds like fun to you, it is at least a way to get some practice pitching.

Some writers' conferences that include pitching to agents give you ten minutes to pitch, and therefore a better chance of impressing them and being remembered. Like contests, you can find these advertised in scriptwriting magazines and on the internet.

Pitching Online

I have been wary of this. It seems like throwing ideas out onto the net would be asking for them to be stolen. But some have seen positive results. The source material for a major network miniseries project I scripted was found by the producer in a pitching chat room, where he met the author of the book. I have also had students who got producers interested in their scripts by pitching them in chat rooms.

Ask for the name, company, and credits of the person you are pitching to. Then look them up. Call the Producers Guild and see if their credits are legitimate. Go to the DVD/video rental store and see if their names are on the jackets of the movies they claim to have produced. Do your homework. Many of these people are legitimate, but it's prudent to be careful.

Having direct interest from a producer is also a great hook for a query letter to an agent.

When They Say "Send It"

This is the first big leap toward your dream coming true. After they ask to read your script, be sure to write "AS REQUESTED" on the outside of the envelope in the lower left-hand corner in bold print so it will stand out from the un-requested slush pile.

Most screenwriters don't include an SASE (self-addressed stamped envelope). It seems amateurish and a little cheap if you're spending $4.00 on stamps to get back a manuscript that costs $7.00 to photocopy. It also implies that either you expect them to reject it, or you are paranoid about it floating around, both of which are not what you want them to think.

Just send the scripts out. Sometimes agents will return them at their own expense. Sometimes they'll keep them. Some scripts just disappear. Think of this process as the Biblical "casting your bread upon the water." Trust that if your script is good enough, your $11 investment (copying plus postage) may come back to you multiplied a hundred thousand times.

Give them a month to read it. And if you haven't heard by then, put in a friendly check-in call. Make note of the assistant's name. Ask if he/she knows of your script and if the agent has read it yet. The assistant can sometimes rescue your script from being deeply buried and move it to the top of the stack.

Signing a Release

It is standard practice in the movie industry not to read unsolicited material without the author first signing a release form indemnifying the producer from any future lawsuits. This protects the production company in the event that they are developing something similar to the script being submitted. The wording in these forms is horrifying. They seem to say that you are giving them the legal right to steal everything you have ever written, or ever will write—and your firstborn child.

Horrendous as they are, in their unadulterated, appalling small print, I'm afraid that there is almost no way around signing release forms if you want producers or development people to read your work before you have an agent. Of course, if you get an agent first, your submissions will be solicited and so release forms will no longer be necessary.

Plagiarism Paranoia

You will have to come to terms with your own fear that everyone is waiting to rip you off. If you have read the trades (*Variety* and *The Hollywood Reporter*), you will already know that even if someone has signed a release, that person can still bring a lawsuit if his/her material is stolen.

This kind of theft is rare. In the years I've worked in the industry I've heard of only a handful of legitimate cases of scripts being stolen.

It is a misconception that the only thing Hollywood is looking for is a great idea. Every would-be producer has ideas galore. People are pitching stories and ideas by the hundreds. What the industry is looking for is not just a good story. It is looking for a terrific writer. Someone who can deliver a wonderful script from which they can make a great movie. Even a sensational idea can make a lousy movie if it is not executed well.

Never send out a rough draft of anything. You don't want people thinking, "What a good idea. Too bad she couldn't pull it off." If *you* pull it off, you won't have to worry about getting ripped off.

Paranoia in the screenwriting biz is a sure sign you're an amateur. You may not be able to stop feeling it, but don't talk about it. Don't worry, your script is registered. If they steal it, you'll sue them and win.

Repeat this affirmation: "I can write better, faster, and cheaper. They'd be fools to use anybody else."

Who Will Be Reading It?

Once you have sent your script off to a producer, studio executive, or agent, who will actually be reading it? The chances are rather good—unless you are well connected to someone higher up—that the first person to be "covering" your script will be a staff reader, someone's assistant, or even someone paid a small fee ($50 or so per script) to read and write a one-page synopsis and critical evaluation. This page is called "coverage." Sometimes these readers are film students, or English grad students, or even hopeful screenwriters trying to keep food on the table until they can sell one of their own.

The reader, after synopsizing the storyline, will evaluate the writing and then label it either (a) Not Recommended, (b) Recommended, or (c) Highly Recommended. It is usually only the "highly recommended" scripts that are read by the higher-ups. In a movie studio, the reading sequence would be first the reader, then a junior-level executive, and then a senior-level executive. At an agency, it might be a reader, followed by an agent's assistant, followed by the agent himself—though often in agencies they skip the middle step. Similarly for a producer, although the number of readings depends on how large the company is. At each level, obviously, the script is only moved up if it is considered an exciting, promising work.

How Long Does It Take for a Script to Be Read?

This varies. If people are excited about it and if the script is known to have been submitted simultaneously to other producers or studios, you might get a positive response very quickly, in a matter of days. This is rare, but it does happen. The fastest response I have had was on a spec feature script that was submitted to a handful of producers late Friday morning for the "weekend read." At 4:30 that same afternoon, my agent called to say that one of them had already read it, loved it, and "wanted to acquire it." Exciting, yes—but this has happened to me only once.

Producers and agents have enormous piles of scripts to read. Their first obligation is to read their own clients, any scripts they have commissioned to be written, and those for which they have studio or shooting deadlines. (They will probably also promote to the top of the reading pile any scripts by writers already known to them.) A typical reading time for an average submission is two to four weeks.

But don't give up heart if it's taking a long time. A few years ago I was having dinner at a friend's house where an agent was present. He made an offhand remark about how there weren't many talented young screenwriters around, whereupon I found myself, quite unexpectedly, pitching him a script two of my students had just written. It was funny and fresh and a cute premise. He loved the story and asked me to have them send it to him, which they promptly did. It took him four months to get around to reading it. When he finally did, he signed them immediately and within two weeks had sold their script for a quarter of a million dollars. Sometimes it actually happens this way. The script became *Don't Tell Mom the Babysitter's Dead* and launched their writing careers.

Follow-Up Calls

The general rule: it's fine to follow up, but give them at least three weeks to read before you call. How should you act? What should you say? How can you get through to the right person?

First, you call the agent/studio/producer, get connected to the right office through the switchboard if there is one. Never call between 12:30 and 2:30 p.m.—everyone in Los Angeles is at lunch then. Don't call before 9:30 a.m. or after 7 p.m. These are typical working hours of the industry.

Always find out the assistant's name when you call the first time. Make a note of it in your Rolodex so that the next time you call, you can use it like this:

JANE'S VOICE: Mr. Thalberg's office.
ME: Hi, Jane. It's Cynthia Whitcomb.

And so on. You can ask how her vacation was or if Mr. T is back from Cannes, etc. Better than the total stranger call, yes? It's always to your advantage to have someone's assistant as an ally. She can be enormously helpful. She can supply you with information ("He should be back from Cannes on the fifteenth"), check on where your script is, retrieve it if it's lost, or even read it herself and put in a good word for you. Also, quite often assistants go on to become agents, producers, or executives in their own right. They may recall favorably those who treated them like intelligent, important people when they were still underlings.

Should I Pay Someone to Read My Script?

There are services that advertise that if you send in your script and a reading fee of several hundred dollars (or more!) they will give you a professional evaluation. If it's good enough, they say they will try to get it to the right people. I don't recommend this—unless it's a writing teacher you know to be good, you're still in your student stage, and the fee is reasonable. As a way into the business, it's a waste of money. If they were well-connected in the Industry, would they be reading scripts for a living?

If you want an unbiased opinion of someone in the business, ask an assistant to send you a copy of the coverage their company did on your script. Assure him or her that you won't tell anyone she did, but that as a writer it will be valuable to you to learn where you are missing the mark. You don't have to take the coverage seriously. Some coverage is brilliant, some collegiate, and some just plain stupid. Remember: everything that happens to you is an opportunity to learn and to move a step closer to your goal.

Do Everything You Can to Move Your Career Forward!

People who make it are the ones who do what it takes to succeed. Every "Breaking In" story is different. In fact, there is a book called *The First Time I Got Paid for It*, which is a compilation of Breaking In stories from about 50 successful screenwriters, and they are all completely different. Obviously there is no single magic door. There are hundreds—most of them closed most of the time. In order to find the right door that will open for you at the right moment, you have to try every knob, bell, and knocker—everything.

Of course, I mean only those things that fall within the law and within your own personal code of morality and ethics. Get creative. Ask yourself this question on a daily basis "What else could I be doing to move my career forward?" Make lists of things you could do. Write those letters. Make those phone calls. Send out another copy. Try another lead.

You may (or may not) be surprised that the biggest thing that stops people at this stage is not exhaustion or despair or frustration. It is fear of embarrassment. Asking for something from a complete stranger who owes you nothing is a daunting task, but after all, this is business.

Remember that nearly every person you are asking for help was probably once in your position. You belong to a long, glorious tradition of young, talented, struggling artists. You may never look back on this time and laugh, but it definitely will make what follows in the years to come taste sweeter by comparison.

This is the time to gather your courage. You have already shown that you have the guts to stick to the long and lonely process of writing and polishing an entire screenplay. The kind of courage that is necessary now is the kind it takes to call someone again after they have already refused to return your call half a dozen times. Or to send them another screenplay after they have already rejected or ignored your first or second or third. It is the inexhaustible determination to pull yourself up by the bootstraps and try again and again and again.

A couple of years ago, a young writer I know started a campaign in June to get an agent. She took time off from her job and spent a couple of weeks and about $65 on stamps. She wrote query letters to all the agents on the list. Nine of them responded with interest, wanting to read her work. That September she signed her first management contract with a good agent.

The bottom line is simple. If you are talented and willing to work hard, willing to do everything you possibly can to make it, then the chances are good that you *will* succeed.

CHAPTER 6

The First Deal

There are three basic types of first jobs young writers can expect to get. Your favorite, of course, would be to sell your original screenplay or at least an option on it. There are two other ways that are common. Based on your calling card script, you might be hired to rewrite a screenplay that someone is developing. Third, and most common, is to be hired to develop a new screenplay for a company. This is called a "development deal." In this arrangement they pay you, in installments, to write a script under their supervision.

Selling a Screenplay

Probably one reason that you are out there writing a screenplay is that you've heard those thrilling tales of people who have written their first script and sold it for a million dollars. This does happen, of course.

Some of you may have heard the quote that it is more likely a person will win $1 million playing the lottery than selling a screenplay. This is foolishly misrepresenting the truth. Those statistics are created by the simple observation that more people win $1 million in the lottery every year than sell scripts for $1 million. But hundreds of millions of lottery tickets are sold, and only tens of thousands of scripts are written, and most of those are never even submitted. So scratch that urban myth off your memory pad. It ain't true.

But the million-dollar sale itself can also be misleading. When *Variety* reports that a spec script sold for a million dollars, amazingly, it does not always mean that the writer was paid a million dollars for a screenplay. What? How can that be? Take my hand and follow me. I hate to burst your favorite bubble, but you need to know the truth.

Like development deals, script sales have payments spread out over time. It usually depends on the film being shot, and the original writer getting sole screenplay credit, in order for the entire sales price to be paid out to the writer. The Million Dollar sale may actually pay a lot less than that.

The breakdown for selling a screenplay quoted in *Variety* as being a $1,000,000 sale might be as follows:

Option for a year (paid immediately)	$150,000
First set of revisions	$125,000
Second set of revisions	$125,000
Polish	$100,000
Bonus on shooting film	$500,000
Total sale	$1,000,000

This means that if they don't shoot it, you'd only be paid $500,000 instead of $1,000,000. Even though a million is the quoted sale price. Also remember that if they don't like the first set of revisions, they can hire someone else to come in and rewrite it without paying you more than the first two installments, which total $275,000. If they shoot it and you share credit with this new writer, your bonus money would be cut in half and only come to $250,000. Now the total sale comes to $525,000. This isn't bad. But it also isn't $1,000,000. My point is that the million-dollar sales figures that are thrown around are often misleading.

Options

Optioning a screenplay means "the buyer" has the exclusive right to try to develop the project for the length of time fixed by the option period. During this time you cannot try to sell it elsewhere. Obviously, you don't give someone an option if there is a lot of activity from companies interested in buying it. But if you've got enthusiasm from a strong producer or if only one person has expressed interest, an option might be a good opportunity for you.

Options can be as short as 30 days, if someone just wants you to hold off while they try and close a deal for it somewhere, or as long as 18 months. The Writers Guild (WGA) minimum for an option is 18 months for 10% of the minimum screenplay sale price. That would translate into numbers (for early 2002) between $4,800 and $9,000. It could be higher, of course. This fee is negotiated by your agent.

In actual practice, if you are not yet a member of the WGA, a producer will often offer a much smaller sum to option a screenplay. There are legitimate producers that offer writers $10 for a six-month option. For all practical purposes, this is a free option with a bit of money changing hands just to make it more legal. The reason producers might offer so little of course, is that this money is coming out of their own personal pockets. There are times you would be wise to take this deal. The question I'd suggest you ask the producer is "How many projects do you have under option now?" If the producer is hoarding options and has dozens, I'd think twice about jumping into a pot that's already full. How much attention can that producer give each project if he has 50? On the other hand, if he or she only has a handful, that is different. You don't want to let your hot new script get cold, dog-eared, and shopworn with no one even going to bat for it to give it its best shot.

At the end of the option, the producer usually has the right to renew the option or negotiate to buy the script. If he does not renew it, *all* rights revert to you, the writer.

Rewrite Jobs

The word "rewrite" in Hollywood refers to the process of one writer revising another writer's screenplay for pay. Making changes in your own script as part of a deal, is called "Revisions," "Polish," or simply "Second Draft," "Third Draft," etc.

Studios sometimes hire new writers for rewrites when they have already used up most of their development money on the first writer, but need more changes made for less money. Left with few alternatives, they will sometimes take a chance on a new writer.

I used to see, at some of the better restaurants in the valley, a white Rolls Royce with the license plate REWRITE. It was a gleaming testimony to the fact that script doctors can make extremely sweet money.

WGA minimum in 2002 for a feature screenplay rewrite (i.e., for the big screen) with a budget of over $5,000,000 (and few studios can make a movie for less) is $25,232. That is the minimum wage for this job. Star rewriters can make six figures a week doing this. Like the song says, nice work if you can get it. The amount of time you are given to rewrite a script varies depending on how drastic a job it is. The average time might be four weeks.

There is also something called the "Page One Rewrite." This means they want the writer to start from scratch using the same basic source material. They pay you less than they would if you were the first writer doing exactly the same amount of work.

The issue of credit arbitration is covered later in Chapter 15, but you should know that in a Page One Rewrite, there is still a good chance that the original writer will share the credit with you—even if there is not one word left of the original screenplay. So don't be too disappointed later. The system is designed to protect a writer from having his work completely taken away. The feeling at the Writers Guild is that the first writer was the one who started it and should still be acknowledged in some way. This same bias could later benefit you.

Development Deals

Face it, these days the major studios develop and buy more than 50 screenplays for every one that is filmed. These odds are lousy—it is a crapshoot. But long before you realize that the script they were so excited about may die on the shelf, you have gone on to development heaven, or hell, or purgatory, depending on how you look at it. You are making development deals one right on the heels of another, with checks coming in regularly, and story meetings alternating with lunches where you pitch ideas to set up the next deals before the current ones are even written.

It is easy to get caught up in the carnival atmosphere with barkers on every side competing for you. When you've had no work for so long, the intoxication of being sought after, wined, dined, wooed, and flattered is very heady. Like many of my students after me, I spent a year or two in making deals, taking meetings, and developing ideas without producing any good solid screenplays. You need to get off the merry-go-round, clear your head, and continue to develop as a *writer*, or one day the music suddenly stops, you crash and burn, no one will return your calls, and you have to begin all over again.

Generally your first development deal (also called a "step deal") will probably be for minimum WGA wage or close to it. Minimums for feature-length theatrical screenplays increase every six months (negotiated by the WGA), but in 2002, the WGA minimums are as follows:

Screenplay for a low-budget film (under $5 million): $50,444
Screenplay for a high-budget film (over $5 million): $94,698

These are the minimums. Your agent will start negotiating here and will hopefully (and usually) get better than minimum. This money is not paid in one lump sum. It is divided up in more or less the following way. The breakdown is somewhat negotiable in the contract. If you need more money in advance, your agent can ask for it. But a typical breakdown for a script might look like this:

Commencement of services	10%
Delivery of story (outline)	15%
Advance on first draft	25%
Delivery of first draft	25%
Commencement of second draft	10%
Delivery of second draft	10%
Delivery of polish	5%

This is just a sample breakdown, but it is typical. So even though the deal you made sounds like a lot of money, no one check you receive will probably amount to more than a quarter of the total. The good thing to note, though, is that you might get as much as half of the money before you've written the script.

Another condition to be aware of: in first deals there may be a cut-off clause. This means that if you deliver the story outline and they don't like the way you've laid it out, they can terminate the deal after having paid you only the advance and delivery of story money, or approximately 25%. Then depending on how the contract was negotiated, they may own your original story and hire another writer to do the screenplay.

You should know, as you make your first deal, that studios and producers are not always prompt in paying. This is not like working at the corner supermarket where you work the week and pick up your check on Friday. This is freelance writing for companies that generally have a lot of paperwork and red tape. Once you turn your script in, the average amount of time before you receive payment for it is two to three weeks.

First your agent has to bill the film company. Then they have to request payment from Payroll, get it on the computer, get the check cut, and send it to your agent. He then takes his 10% and sends you another check for 90%. It is not unusual for this process to take a month. Be aware of this, so you can avoid the stress of rushing in a script on Friday afternoon hoping to get a check in time to meet the mortgage payment by Monday—or lose the house. It just doesn't work that quickly.

A note about your checks. While we're on the subject, it's a good idea to go into your bank once you have a development deal, and introduce yourself to the bank manager. Tell him or her that you're a freelance writer and will be getting paychecks from time to time for rather large amounts of money, always from your agent's bank. This is your salary and you would appreciate it if he or she could okay your checks when they come in so that they can be immediately credited to your account. When you wait close to a month for a nice check, and run to your bank—only to have a teller put a hold on it for eight to ten working days for it to clear, it can drive you *nuts*.

The Contract

In addition to how much money they will pay you to write, your contract covers a lot of other things which you should be aware of. They can be 20 pages long or more, and in amazingly small print. Here is a checklist of what should be covered:

☑ **How much money.** Of course. (See above.)

☑ **How much time for each step of the deal.** This means how much time you have to write, but also how much time they have to read each step. You don't want to turn in the first draft and wait months for them to come back with notes. Time is money. And they have to get back to you within a reasonable time frame. Often this is around four weeks.

☑ **Sequels.** If a theatrical or television sequel is made, you as the writer of the original script need to be paid for that. And it needs to be included in the contract. You can't assume anything. Many hit movies have had television movie sequels. *Butch Cassidy,* for instance, had *Mrs. Sundance.* Part of that money needs to go to the screenwriter, and the studio owns the copyright on the script. So it gets included in the contract. Along with:

☑ **Remakes.** In 20 years, if they remake your movie with the next hot young stars, you need to make sure you will be paid.

☑ **Television Series.** *M*A*S*H** was a movie before it made zillions of dollars as a popular (and now syndicated) television series. Your contract should include this paragraph. Your royalty on a TV series based on your screenplay might typically be $2,000 per episode for a half-hour show, or $3,500 per episode for a one-hour dramatic series. You may also be able to negotiate here, that any future television series would have to award you a "Created By" credit, which can literally be worth millions of dollars if the series runs seven years and goes into syndication.

☑ **Novelization.** If your screenplay becomes a major motion picture, it is likely also to become a paperback book. If you want to do this yourself, you need it in your contract up front. David Seltzer wrote the novelization of *The Omen,* based on his original screenplay, and may have made even more money for the book than he did for the script. He took the time to write it well, and it went to the top of the bestseller lists. Even if you don't want to write the book, you should have it in your contract that you get part of the profits from the book.

☑ **Soundtracks.** Usually the writer doesn't have a piece of the soundtrack, but there are cases where you should negotiate for that. If you had written *Almost Famous,* for instance, creating an imaginary rock band, with a style and characters, and that imaginary band went on to have a hit album in the real world, shouldn't you as creator of that band, have a piece of that? The special DVD version of *Almost Famous* includes the Stillwater album CD.

☑ **Franchising.** If your movie is for kids, or has a unique, recognizable character that can be franchised, you should get part of that. Melissa Mathison, who wrote the screenplay for *E.T.*, created a new, unique creature that went onto T-shirts, lunchboxes, dishes, sheets, kids' underwear, in addition to little plastic guys being tucked into Happy Meals all over the world. If you made up the character on which these toys are based, you should have a piece of that as well. So make sure your agent negotiates for a percentage of this.

These are examples of some of the things your contract should cover. Which is one reason you don't want an attorney from your hometown who is not an entertainment attorney negotiating your contract. He wouldn't know what to ask for. And you don't want to pay for his education at an hourly rate. Get an agent.

Revising Your Own Work

The chances of a studio (or anyone else) buying your original screenplay and shooting it word for word are almost nil. They will want changes. They will have other ideas about how things should be. It is typical of a first writer, especially one who has just had a script validated by a large, glamorous sale, to be emotionally attached to the script as written. More experienced writers can be attached too, of course. But they know that if you don't make the changes "required," the executives will hire someone else who will. While changing your beloved screenplay can be painful, it is nothing compared to the feeling of having a stranger mess it up beyond recognition—and get paid your money for doing it!

I shall go into more details about strategies for protecting your script in Chapter 14 (Story Meetings), but I want to make a few key points about it now while we're getting prepared for the first job.

Adapting to Changes

If in your mind the script is finished, bronzed like your baby shoes, it could stop the creative process. True, it may be worthy of Cameron Crowe, but I strongly doubt that there is absolutely no way you could improve upon it.

While you are deeply entrenched in the part of your deal called "revisions," one of three things will happen: You will make it better, you will make it worse, or you will just make it different, with no improvements, feeling that you are wasting your time, merely pacifying those in power with meaningless reshuffling.

I suggest that the only way you will be happy in the process is if you find ways to improve your script. Make it your serious, committed task to find those things you can do to make the script better, and do them. The people who are paying you and giving you notes sometimes do come up with ideas that will help. They often say things that trigger other ideas in you. So don't spend your time in these meetings defending what you have written. If you're defensive about your work, their natural response will be to attack it in order to make their point and to get you to change it. You can explain something that they aren't understanding, but don't try to tell them why something they don't like is good. This can get unpleasant rather quickly. Spend the time wholeheartedly searching for ways to make a good script better.

Never forget that it is already a good script. This is an unstated assumption on the part of all. If they didn't think it was a good script, none of you would be sitting there. They wouldn't be paying you or wasting their time.

If you can find nothing in their notes that you feel can possibly help your script, and you can't get them to buy any of the ideas you come up with, and you are forced into the corner of writing it the way they want it even though you feel deeply that it is hurting the script, you must remember: movie making is called "the Industry" for a reason. It's a business. It is also a job.

Your goal in life used to be to sell a screenplay, to become a professional, and you have finally done that. You have sold your script. It is theirs now. The heart of the creative process is the first draft, during which you were able to do exactly what you wanted, to please yourself. Now that part is over.

We are not solitary artists, like painters. You cannot hang a screenplay on a gallery wall. It does not stand alone. It needs to be filmed and brought to life by actors, camera, lights, and sound. It is a collaborative medium.

I know that directors often take credit for work where writers are the true source. But at this point, when they have the big guns and you are clinging to a sinking script (to mangle a few metaphors), it is time to compromise. It is one of the things you are being paid for. And it is partly why you are being paid more than practically anybody in your high school graduating class. This game is hardball; you have to be willing to play hard and by the rules. One of the rules is that once they buy a script, it belongs to them. If you want to keep working on it, you must give them some version of what they ask you for.

It's like being an architect and builder. You design and construct a house that you hope to sell for a handsome profit. The house looks great on the outside, but inside some of the final touches haven't been made. Then someone buys your house and hires you to stay on to put in the lighting fixtures and wallpaper. You will always be credited as the architect. You conceived, designed, and built it, and it will always be yours in your heart. But you had better put up the kind of wallpaper the owner chooses.

CHAPTER 7

Agents

Having an agent is a necessary ingredient for a screenwriting career. Even if you get a producer interested on your own, don't go anywhere near a contract without an agent. If your scripts are terrific and you continue to send them out along with query letters, follow-up letters, and phone calls, sooner or later an agent will want to meet you.

A Typical First Meeting

The agent will want to get to know you. But primarily he or she wants to know what else have you written and what else you want to write. What kind of shape are your other scripts in? What are they about? How soon could they be ready to send out? What is your vision for your career? Only features? Would you consider television?

While they are asking questions and getting to know you, they are also trying to figure out if you are someone they want to work with. Do you have a chip on your shoulder? Are you going to be whining or winning? Difficult or a joy to work with? They are also trying to guess how good you might be at pitching your stories to producers.

At the end of this first meeting, which might last from 30 to 60 minutes, the agent will usually get right to the point about what is next. This exchange might sound something like one of the following:

> "Thanks for coming in. Good-bye." In which case, assuming you like the agent, you say, "Would it be all right if I send you the new script when it's finished?"

> "Let me talk it over with my associates. I'll get back to you." In which case you can also use the response in the example above.

"Keep in touch with me. Let me see the new script when it's ready." You say, "I will. It should be ready in a couple of weeks."

"Well, let me send this script around and see if I can get some interest in it and then we'll see what happens." This is great. Give it some time. Four to six weeks anyway.

"I want to represent you. I'll have my assistant send you a management contract. Read it over and sign it as soon as possible." This rarely happens at a first meeting, but it can.

Generally when you begin a relationship with an agent, it is casual for the first few months. By casual I mean without a formal written contract. The signing of a management agreement with an agency usually happens around the time of signing the first contract for a screenplay.

One reason for this is that it is more difficult to sell a new writer. It sometimes takes quite a while. An agent and a writer need a chance to get to know one another over time and under pressure to see if their personalities will blend or clash. If the chemistry's still good at the end of the first negotiation, there's plenty of time to sign the agency contract then.

Another reason for this delay in signing is that once you've signed with an agent, you may feel free to call and harass him daily to find out what's happening with your career. If he's sending your script out, but is not officially your agent, you will probably be more grateful and less of a phone pest.

The main point is, if an agent doesn't ask you to sign a management contract right away, don't worry. This is how it usually goes.

Formalities

The agent/writer contract. Management contracts vary some, depending on the agency, but there are a few terms that are fairly standard.

Duration. The length of a writer's first contract with an agency might be only one year, but subsequent contracts are usually two to three years. The contract is renewable if both parties wish to sign on for another term. It can be terminated by the writer, if the agent fails to get at least an offer of work at WGA minimum in any 90-day period.

Fees. Standard agent's fees for writers are 10% of your gross off the top. When a check comes in to the agency for you, your agent gets 10% (before taxes) and you get the rest. You will sign an additional page on your contract authorizing your agent to receive each of your checks, cash them, and write another check to you for 90% of the gross amount.

Expenses. Generally, Hollywood agencies will pay for copying your scripts, and postage and messenger service as well, once your career gets rolling. But if it is a smaller literary agency and you are brand new, they may ask you for ten copies of your script to get things started.

When you go to lunch with your agent, who is expected to pick up the tab? Larger agencies usually give their agents expense accounts for taking clients to lunch. If you suspect that lunch might be at your agent's personal expense, you can offer to pick it up. Also, who suggested lunch in the first place? Usually the one who invites, pays.

Remember, too, that your agent knows exactly how much money you make. If you are between jobs, offering to pick up the check will be a transparently noble gesture.

Do I Need a Manager?

Writers' managers, like actors', usually get 15%. I am in the camp that feels that writers don't really need managers, unless they are also directors, actors, or best-selling book authors with publicity tours and speaking gigs to set up. For those of us who are primarily interested in being screenwriters, an agent is sufficient management.

How About an Entertainment Attorney?

A few writers use attorneys specializing in entertainment law to negotiate their contracts for them. This is fine, if for some reason you prefer lawyers to agents. (There is a bad joke in here somewhere.) Many agents are also lawyers. (Mine is.) And all of the bigger agencies have a legal department with plenty of lawyers. If you hire an attorney rather than an agent in the hopes of saving money, good luck. It is a gamble. If I were paid $500 an hour, speed would not be my top priority.

I have had two experiences of lawyers stretching deal negotiations longer than two years. More than 24 months! Just to make a *deal*. Someone's kids were being put through college, and they weren't mine.

One last argument in favor of agents over attorneys: Once a deal is done, an agent is much more likely to find you the next one.

The Agencies

I started out with a small, prestigious literary agency that had half a dozen agents and less than a hundred writers on its list. That particular agency, Adams, Ray & Rosenberg, went on to merge with two larger companies and no longer exists as such. I am now with one of the big three agencies, so I can talk about the advantages and disadvantages of both types from personal experience.

The Big Three

There are dozens of small boutique-type agencies, usually started by a very successful agent from a larger company who decided to go into business for herself, for example. And several mid-size agencies. But most of the power players and energy are in the biggest three agencies. (See Appendix F for contact information.)

CAA (Creative Artists Agency). Even in the post-Michael Ovitz era, CAA is a force to be reckoned with. It was once generally regarded to be the most powerful and prestigious agency in town, but is now on an equal footing with the other two giants.

ICM (International Creative Management). Has been competing with CAA for top dog status for years. Agents in high positions in these companies sometimes move from one to another as they gain power. Both have many stars and large packaging departments.

William Morris. More than 100 years old and legendary. Can still compete in every way. I was at ICM for a dozen years. When my agent defected to Morris, I followed him, so I'm currently here.

UTA (United Talent Agency). It is the fourth largest agency, and in a few years could be on a par with the first three.

One of the advantages to going with a huge agency is that they can pass your script directly to a top producer, director, or actor without leaving the building.

New Agencies

It is often easier to find a crack in the door at a new agency that is still trying to carve out a place for itself and create a sizable client list. The obvious advantage is that they are hungry for clients, while established agents and young hot ones usually already have a full list.

These agents are usually experienced, having broken away from other agencies to form their own companies. Relationships they forged in the industry while working for those other agencies will still help them, and you, now.

Packaging

This is when an agency marries several clients, such as a producer or director or star to a screenplay, or any combination thereof. The project then becomes an agency package. Packaging is a great reason to be at one of the bigger agencies. They have star clients with whom a screenplay could be very happily wed. The two advantages of packaging are first, a much better chance of your screenplay actually being filmed. And second, if your agent packages your script, they take their percentage from the producer or director, or charge a packaging fee directly to the studio, and not from you. So in essence your price just went up ten percent.

Packaging can be a disadvantage, however, if your agency feels your script is strong and wants to use it to boost the career of one of their producer or director clients whose career is floundering. It is possible for a script to remain unsold because any of the elements in the package are not so hot. Remember that just because your agent wants to package you with someone who has already read the script and loves it, you don't have to agree. You have the right to say no to a package proposal if you are unhappy with any of the elements involved.

The Young Hotshot versus the Grand Old Man with Clout

Each of these two (oversimplified) types of agents has advantages:

The Grand Old Man with Clout

He knows everyone in town.

He has the respect of his peers because he doesn't send them junk. He has taste and doesn't handle anyone except the Truly Talented and everybody knows it.

People owe him favors.

He is tough and experienced and if the barracudas come after you, he is able to fend them off and steer you into safer waters.

He has patience, sees the long-range view and will not panic and dump you if you have a dry spell or go into rehab.

He is fatherly, often wise, sometimes warm and encouraging. It feels great to get his approval.

The downside is these guys sometimes keel over on the golf course.

The Young Hotshot

He has enthusiasm and tons of energy.

He moves quickly.

He has no ego problem about calling someone a second time even though they didn't return his first call.

He sometimes negotiates like a maverick, unconcerned with what the "going rate" is, occasionally asking for an outrageous sum on a hunch—and sometimes getting it.

He often is more open to your ideas about what you want to do in your career, without thinking of you in the narrow box of "the kind of thing you do." For instance, if you want to direct, a young hotshot would probably make a better grandstand play to fight for your chance to do so than a more conservative agent who is too aware of the slimness of such a possibility.

Downside: you could lose him if he gets promoted to head of production at Paramount. Or goes into rehab himself.

Choosing the Agent Who's Right for You

Now that you have an idea of what these types of agents might be like, and the agencies they work for, how do you choose an agent?

First of all, you decide which type of agency feels more like you, and then pursue agencies of that type.

If you have sent your script out to many agents, and two or more are pursuing you, how do you know which one you should go with? If all are of about equal strength or their differing strengths balance each other, a choice can be difficult. I recommend you select one based on the three most important criteria:

Genuine enthusiasm. Which one do you feel honestly believes you to be the most talented, remarkable writer? They may flatter you profusely, but you have a built-in crap detector, and if you listen closely, a bell will go off when someone is handing you a load of bull. Choose the one who means it. Or means it more. You want the agent that will be able to promote you honestly as the latest and greatest writer in town.

Personality. Often an agent will be enthusiastic, influential, and good at his job, but will be intimidating to a new writer. One case in point:

One of my students, a brilliant, shy girl just over 20, wrote a terrific spec script for a hit comedy series. People got excited about it and before she knew it she was getting offers to do sitcoms and TV movies. Someone introduced her to an agent who was one of the grandest of the Grand Old Men. It was a real coup to be signed by him, but she was badly intimidated around him.

She was a neophyte. There were a lot of things she needed to know about the business, but he didn't have time to teach her, or interest. He had taken her on as a favor to a friend. He agreed that she was talented, but had no personal enthusiasm for her work. She couldn't get through to him on the phone to ask things she needed to know.

When problems arose between the young writer and her employers who were old-timers, her agent would apologize for his naïve client and agree with them that she was inexperienced and difficult. Happily, she had the gumption to break away from this agent and find someone more right for her.

You need to be able to relax and talk honestly with your agent. To feel free to ask any questions you need answers to. Maybe an agent is too abrasive, or gushing and phony, or just gets on your nerves. If the agent believes in you and is working hard on your behalf, some of these traits you can learn to live with. But sometimes it's just not the right match.

Intuition. For me, the intuitive, gut feeling about someone usually turns out to be the decisive factor. You can almost always trust your instincts in this kind of choice. One will always feel more right than the other. If you really can't decide, close your eyes and imagine walking into each of their offices, sitting down and talking about your career. Then ask yourself—in which daydream do you feel happiest?

Changing Agents

Your relationship with your agent is like a marriage in some ways, but it is not necessarily made for life. Your contract is up every two years and you have the choice of signing again or leaving.

I was with my first agents for 12 years, which was all of my adult life. I thought I would never change agents, because I loved them and they were very good at their jobs. But at a certain point I realized that they no longer shared my own vision for my career. I was a successful TV movie writer. I was on all the networks' lists of approved writers and was hired over and over again. I was making close to top money for those jobs and as far as they were concerned, that was fine. In their view, I should go on writing three TV movies a year and be happy.

The problem was there were lots of other things I wanted to write: features, miniseries, books, plays, pilots, musicals. TV movies were only a small part of what interested me.

It's easy for an agent to continue to get a writer work in an arena where she's already proved herself. Trying to promote a writer in a new arena where the writer has no credentials or experience is hard work. The agent has to actually fight for you. He has to call people and pitch you for projects. Send out scripts. Exert a lot of energy. And there's no guarantee that the writer will succeed in this new area. My first agency didn't have any interest in expanding my writing career. They had recently merged into a much larger agency, and had other things on their mind. I was one of the steady "meat and potatoes" clients who could be counted on to do a steady business for the company each year. This merger (creating Triad Artists) also meant that there were a lot of new agents suddenly representing me who had never even met me or read my work. The feeling I got from the last meeting I had at this agency, between me and six agents, was that they saw me as a talented kid they had taken in and developed a successful career. And that I should be grateful for it and not be a problem.

So I left them (somewhat tearfully) and went with a young hotshot who thought of me as a star in my field with potential to do whatever I wanted to do; he showed a gung-ho willingness to back my ambitions for my own career with all of his phenomenal energy and smarts. How did I know he was good? At our first get-acquainted meeting he asked me to send over some scripts so he could read my work. I said "How many scripts do you want?" He asked how many I'd written. At the time it was something over 40. He asked me to pick my favorite seven and send them. I sent them over. He read all seven of them over the weekend and we talked about all of them on Monday. He reads! That sold me right there.

In the first year of being with this new agent (who will remain nameless so you guys don't swamp him), he got me $100,000 more for a feature-film development deal than I had ever gotten before, plus producing credits in television, a miniseries that got me an Emmy nomination, and a book deal.

If you are considering changing agents, start putting out feelers. Tell people you know in the industry that you're thinking about going somewhere else. Soon agents will be calling you, or people will be referring you to agents they know. You can meet a few and decide if they are better than what you've got. If not, you can always stay where you are. Just be careful where you meet with new agents. If you end up deciding to stay with your first agent after all, you don't need her angry because she saw you at The Ivy shopping around.

The only thing I caution you about is "agent hopping." Writers who change agents every two years seem flaky and basically unhappy. Also, it makes it harder for potential employers to track you down.

Can I Leave My Agent Before My Contract Is Up?

Legally you are obligated to stay with your current agent until your contract has expired, unless 90 days have elapsed in which they got you no job offers. But if you are very unhappy and another agency is courting you, arrangements can usually be made to avoid lawsuits and major unpleasantness. Have your new agent renegotiate your deal with your current agents to let you go. Normally, your former agents will continue to get commission on all work they obtained for you and a diminishing percentage of commissions on new work you do for the length of the old contract. The two legal departments of the two agencies will work it out between them, and you will then be free to work with the new agent.

Be cordial in these dealings. Your old agency is not legally obligated to release you. You signed a contract to stay with them for two years. If they do let you go early, you should be grateful for the favor.

Use all this information in combination with whatever you can find out about a specific agent in order to make a sound choice. But I encourage you to let your intuitive, inner voice have the final word.

CHAPTER 8

Who to Work For:
The Producers

Like creatures of the sea, producers come in all varieties. Anyone can call himself a producer. Many of them are sharp, talented people. But others have nothing more than chutzpah for credentials. In this chapter we cover all levels of producers in a brief overview, starting at the top and working our way down.

The Biggies

The biggest producers own their own companies and do any films they want to. They have large amounts of money available and don't need to hook up with the major studios, though often they do. These are people like Spielberg (Dreamworks and Amblin) and Lucas (Lucas Film and Industrial Light and Magic), Rob Reiner (Castle Rock), and Ron Howard (Imagine.) Working for them is very much like working for Fox or Universal.

Producers on the Lots

Many producers have deals to develop movies for major studios. They will often have their offices on the studio lots. They are still independent producers, but Fox (for example) gives them office space and a salary in exchange for first shot at the projects the producer is developing. Producers in this category have at least one successful film under their belts.

If the studio executives turn down a project from one of their producers, the producer can take it to another studio even though his office is at Fox.

The first thing you always want to find out about a producer before you get involved in any deal is what has he or she produced. Do they have any credits? There are many ways to find out. You can call the Producers Guild of America. They have a directory. *The Hollywood Directory* lists them; it is available in book form or on the internet. Some of the published guides to videos list producers as well as actors and directors. (Some even list writers and cinematographers.) Read credits at the beginning and end of movies. Read video cassette and DVD cases. Any producer with a deal at a studio is probably legitimate. You may or may not like his taste, but he has credibility.

Freelance Producers

These usually rank somewhere in the middle of the spectrum. They have their own offices and take their projects to the major studios to try to set them up there. They range from very successful and sought-after names to people still trying to get their first film shot. As always, use their credits as a guideline.

Small Independent Producers

These are generally the more artistic type of film makers who get independent financing and make their movies on lower budgets without going through the big studios. They range from people like James Ivory and Ismail Merchant *(A Room With a View* and *Howard's End)* and John Sayles *(Brother From Another Planet)* to obscure names whose films aren't distributed beyond the art film festivals. I have only written two screenplays for these small, independent companies, but I have many friends and students who have also had experience with them. These companies often have high artistic goals and devote great passion, enthusiasm, and energy toward fulfilling them, but rarely have the money to pay WGA minimums.

The only time a writer should get involved with these companies (for little or no money) is if:

• The project they are throwing themselves behind is your own, beloved screenplay that is so special and out of the mainstream that it would have no little or no chance in the larger marketplace.

• The project they are asking you to do is a story so magnificent, or a book you have loved all your life or something you would have traded your pet dog to have thought of yourself—and you will never forgive yourself if you pass this one up.

• The people involved are of such superb and proven artistic and production ability that it would be a gift from God to have the opportunity to work with them. This means that they are people of the caliber of Merchant/Ivory and John Sayles—people who have won top awards in important categories at major film festivals and you have seen and adored their other films.

• Your ten-year high school reunion is next month and you can't face the question "Are you famous yet?" without being able to say, "I'm writing a screenplay for Phantom Productions."

In these cases, I would recommend getting involved; in all other cases, there is a great likelihood of heartache. Here are some of the things to watch out for when working for these companies.

Writing Against Deferred Payment or a Piece of the Profits

If a writer is not being paid, she should write for herself, to please herself and should own 100% of the rights to what she has written.

These small independent producers have a tendency to make promises they can't keep. They may ask you to write a screenplay based on their idea on spec. This means you put in your labor now on something you do not own (and have no right to sell), on the promise of money, someday. (Maybe.) I know these are sincere people. I know that they believe that this picture will be made, that they will raise the money no matter what.

They may want you to do a quick rewrite of a script they already have that just needs "a little work. You could do it in two weeks." When the picture is made, they'll give you 5% of all the profits and it will make tons of profits because they are going to shoot it for only $300,000 and they know somebody at HBO that is interested in the cable rights based on the story alone. Be careful not to get seduced by these overtures.

A Case in Point

I always credit Tony Bill with giving me my first screenwriting job. The truth is he gave me my first "professional" screenwriting job. I wrote a feature for $1,000 for a small independent producer when I was still an undergrad at UCLA.

He was a Mormon who made small industrial promotional films for a living and desperately wanted to make a "real" movie. What he hired me to write was a "G-rated suspense movie that could be shot for $200,000 and that used three dirt bikes and a tiny Cessna airplane." These were the things they already had and they wanted to maximize their production value. They also knew a beautiful red dirt box canyon near Kanab, Utah, where they wanted to shoot.

From these elements I concocted a story of three high school kids joy-riding on their dirt bikes who tangle with a redneck crazy on a Caterpillar bulldozer who tries to scare them, accidentally kills one kid, then traps the other kids in a dead-end canyon.

I've heard much worse accounts of first deals, but in this one I got paid in $50 and $100 installments spread out over a couple of years, when I would call and beg. The picture did get made. I went to the "premiere" in a tiny theater in a small town where the producer/director lived. It was definitely rated G. In fact, they whitewashed all the suspense out of it. The first kid that got killed turned out not to be dead after all, just stunned. Whenever the suspense built up, the characters would stop and pray at length. Well, it was so bad that I had them use a pseudonym instead of my real name. But it was academic, because the movie was never released.

Another Case

I knew a completely honest and sincere (though not very experienced) independent producer who raised the money he needed to make a low-budget feature in $5,000 increments from friends and relations. He personally guaranteed that everyone would, at the very least, get their money back. He even used his home as collateral. Then the film ran over budget. The money dried up, and the producer was sentenced to 21 months in prison for fraud. I hope he got off early for good behavior. He was not a criminal by most definitions, but last I heard he was sitting in a medium-security facility in Orange County.

Rewriting for the Independents

A less extreme case is when an independent producer asks you to make changes in your own script, without reimbursement, to make it more attractive to their "money people." I suggest that you do this only if you sincerely feel that the changes improve your script and, of course, if all concerned are clear that all rights to it still belong to you.

I can't tell you how many times new writers come to me, excited about these independent movie deals, and tell me that even though there's no money now, they know there will be because *this* one's going to get made.

If you think the odds of getting a film made at a major studio are lousy, they are terrific compared to these outfits. I don't have any hard statistics, but my guess is that one in a thousand of these projects actually gets shot and released.

I know how tempting it is to get involved with such ever-hopeful undertakings. I know how long and hard you have worked and how badly you need to feel validated and to be a working part of the film industry. If you get involved, be sure you know the score. Don't tell everyone you know that your movie's getting made until your film is in the can. Promised money from these people is not real money until it is safely in your bank account.

The purpose of this warning is to inform you so that you will not be naive and have your dreams smashed. Your vision of your career should be based on a realistic idea of what the industry is like. There is still plenty of room to be excited and inspired because amazing things do happen. In real life. Not in a lot of talk.

I can almost hear the independents screaming, "If she had her way, no creative, original, artistic films could ever get made! We can't survive without artists contributing their services and someone taking risks. There is no art without risk!" To this I respond, "If you want to make films independently, why not find original screenplays, by writers with their own artistic vision and their own voice, and take out a six-month option for a nominal fee?"

Then, during the option, if the producers can get the money people interested enough—based on *your* screenplay—they can pay a reasonable price for the script, commission any rewrites, promise percentages, whatever they want. Then it will be legitimate work for pay; it will be a *professional* arrangement.

Student film projects are another issue; one that I won't go into here. They are essentially non-profit undertakings, and this is a book about your commercial career.

And now: on down to the bottom of the barrel.

The Sleazeballs

There are a few studios that are small-time, not signatory to the Writers Guild, that produce a large number of exploitation movies. I'm not talking about pornography. We're not going to go quite that low. But there is a level, above porn, but below almost everything else. These companies make their money producing slasher-type movies, monster movies, and teenage sex-ploitation movies about high school prostitution.

They prey on film school students. They usually pay about $5,000 to write one of their films and give you a title, a premise, and about four weeks to write it. They choose these titles by surveying teens in malls asking questions such as "Would you see a movie called *The Beast in the Basement*?" They often want to shoot them in foreign countries or on a specific set that they already have. The budgets are always extremely low. Many of my students have taken these jobs because they were there. Five thousand dollars is still a lot more than most students could ever make in a month doing anything legal; and some of them believe they can write a really classy horror film or brilliant new style of horror movie. These companies also lure students in by promising them that if this one works out well, the student may be able to direct the next one.

The writers who think they can do good work for these companies are always badly disappointed. These companies don't want good writing. They want trash. They want it fast and they want it sleazy. Students take these jobs because they believe it will bring them one step closer to where they want to be. But these credits rarely help you in the legitimate movie world.

Another thing to be careful about is getting the money. They often pay slowly. One student of mine finally got his check late in the afternoon before he was planning to take the Red-eye Express home for Christmas. When he got to the studio's bank he found that the check for $5,000 was not good. He raised hell and the producers finally got him enough cash for the flight, but who needs the headaches and ulcers?

If you do choose to make a deal with one of these sleazy companies (and they are easy to spot by their movie ads in the newspaper), make sure your contract states that you can use a pseudonym if you want to. Several of my students have deeply regretted having their names connected in any way with this junk, after they later became known for their own work. Not that anyone who matters sees these movies, but everyone in town reads the ads and having "written by" prominently in the newspapers is bad enough.

The Flakes

There are a huge number of flakes on the fringes of the movie business and a few on the inside. These are people you want to avoid. Here are some ways to spot a Flake.

- They have produced very few, if any, actual movies.
- They lie, and you can usually tell when they are lying.
- They drop names excessively. They tell stories that make themselves sound like Tom Cruise's best friend.
- They do a lot of hanging out at the right places where nothing is really happening. Clubs. Parties. Gyms. The Right Restaurants.
- They tend to wear a lot of expensive jewelry. Designer sunglasses. Space-age cell phones and Palm Pilots. Accessories you have only seen in magazines.
- They talk almost exclusively about deals and people. And are at a loss when it comes to story.

Just remember, there are all kinds of producers at all levels of the business. Your first encounters could be with any of them. If your first experience with a producer happens to be negative, or even devastating, don't let it scare you out of the business. You create the screenplays without which there would be no movies. You are the gold mine everybody else is trying to get rich from. They're the salespeople, packagers, and producers. Never invalidate yourself or your work based on the opinions of any of these people, at any level of the business.

And always remember that if you write for free, write for yourself. Write what you love, the way you want to. And own it. If you are going to sell out, get *paid*!

CHAPTER 9

Keeping Your Spirits Up on the Way to Breaking In

There is a very resonant line** from the movie *Julia* that Julia (Vanessa Redgrave) shouts to Lily (Jane Fonda) as her ocean liner is embarking for Europe: "Work hard! Take chances! Be very, very bold!" I have copied the line onto a piece of paper and hung it above my word processor to keep me going on those cold predawn mornings when I face the blank screen alone.

There are a lot of dry spells and professional frustrations in the life of a screenwriter. For the beginner, the time between setting out to work and seeing your name—12 feet wide on a movie screen—can be very tough to live through. It is lonely; it is difficult to know if what you are doing is any good; and there is so much to learn. What it takes to make it through this stage is vision, enthusiasm, and energy. Here are some of the ways I kept myself going en route to success:

The Competition Is Narrowing

I figured (based on no known statistics) that there were maybe a thousand people somewhere in the United States that were trying to be screenwriters about the same time that I was. By the time I had finished and polished my first 120-page screenplay, probably half of them had already dropped out. It takes a lot of time, effort, and willpower to finish something that extensive for which no one is paying you and which no one will ever berate you or fire you for not finishing.

So now it's down to five hundred. By the time I had finished three screenplays, all full-length, two or three drafts of each, and each one of them had been rejected by a dozen people in the industry, I believed that probably only a hundred or so of that original thousand were still going for it.

When my *tenth* screenplay was rejected by the twelfth person, which meant I had 120 consecutive rejections, without a single acceptance, I knew that I was the only one of that original mythical thousand still standing. At that point, with ten screenplays under my belt, and 999 fewer competitors, I was the single most experienced, dedicated screenwriter that anybody could hire for a new writer's price. I was the best deal in town.

If I had quit after my third script, or my seventh or ninth, I would have had no career as a screenwriter. Instead I've had a great ride. (And 25 movies filmed and millions of dollars made.) It may be a cliché that quitters never win and winners never quit. But for all of us aspiring screenwriters, it is true. Do you hear that, Winners? Take this literally, fearlessly and seriously. Do not quit. No matter what.

If You're Writing Screenplays, You're a Screenwriter

The same vision that helps you to dream up stories and characters for your scripts should also be helping you create the vision of yourself as a writer. Stop saying, "I'm trying to be a screenwriter." You *are* a screenwriter. I know it feels like a lie, but you need to push past the self-doubt. Sooner than you think, you may be sitting in someone's office at a studio where you'll be expected to be a screenwriter. So practice on your friends first.

At 21, I was waiting tables at a Bob's Big Boy hamburger place in Pasadena. If someone referred to me as a waitress, I would correct him. "I'm not a waitress. I just do this for a living. I'm actually a writer." Be careful with your words. They can create your reality on many levels. And the more often you say it, the sooner it will come true. How many times did Pinocchio tell people he was going to become a real boy? So repeat after me: "I *am*."

"See" Your Screenplay as a Real Movie

Walter Hill once made a screenplay deal based on a pitch which was nothing more than a description of a billboard in his imagination. He told the studio executives to imagine Clint Eastwood in a dark alley, sitting on a crate, dirty, sweaty, his undershirt torn and his bare fists bloody, under the title *The Street Fighter*. It turned out to be Charles Bronson instead of Eastwood who played it, and the title was changed to *Hard Times*, but Hill saw it so vividly as a movie that he convinced the studio to buy the idea and let him develop it into a screenplay. It turned out to be his directorial debut as well: an important step in a highly successful career.

Begin to see your screenplay as a real movie now. Picture your ideal actors cast in the lead roles. Mentally create the billboard on Sunset Boulevard, the newspaper ads, and see the clips they would choose for the "Coming Attractions" trailers. What ad line would you write for your film? As we'll discuss in the Chapter 11, coming up with an ad line or selling line before there is even a screenplay can give you a decisive edge.

Don't Let Rejection Stop You

My scripts were rejected more than 120 times before I finally broke through. If all I had heard was "Forget it. Your scripts stink. Get a day job." I might have quit. But I'm telling you that no matter how many times your work has been turned down, if the feedback you are getting with the rejections is, "You have talent, stick with it," believe them and take their advice.

Start a New Screenplay at Once

Probably more than any other technique, this kept me artistically alive during those beginning years. I made a rookie mistake my first time out. I finished my screenplay and sent it out and then waited for the fame and fortune to pour in. I went from the creative high of writing and completion gradually into the slump of disappointment and discouragement. It was hard then, from that low point, to sit down and start a new script. That was the last time I made that mistake. I strongly recommend that you learn from mine and don't make this mistake yourself.

After that first near-disaster, I made it a policy to start work on the next screenplay the day after I sent out all the copies of the last one. I mean the very next day, even if starting it only means making notes, doing research, scribbling on a few scene cards.

A writer's instinct may be to take a break at this point and wait for the response to the last one. Days turn into weeks, which turn into months. Don't put it off. Each day you delay starting a new script just makes it that much harder to get back into the pattern of writing.

If you go back to work immediately on a new script, by the time you've been rejected by five or six people, you'll be close to halfway through the new one. Then you can cheer yourself—and rightly so—with the thought, "They didn't want to buy the last script, but the new one will knock them out." Almost all new writers get progressively better with each script they write.

Don't Set Time Limits

I knew a lot of people in college who set themselves deadlines for trying to break in as screenwriters before falling back on something else. They almost invariably gave themselves five years. Not one of those people has made it in the profession.

My position was "I am a screenwriter. Sooner or later someone is going to pay me for this and make my movies. I will hold this intention no matter what it takes or how long." No alternatives. Nothing to fall back on. I decided to write movies as if my life depended on it. To quote The Boss, "No retreat, baby. No surrender."

Setting a time limit is like programming the subconscious mind to fail—and five years is the scheduled failure date. Plan instead for success: *Failure is just another word for quitting.*

The Road Goes Only to Success

Some people see success and failure as two separate but equal forces, opposites, like good and evil. "If you fail you are not a success." This is nonsense. Successful people still fail, and more often than you imagine. The truth is that everyone who has ever succeeded has failed many times.

Think of it this way. You are on a road that leads only to success. If you keep moving forward on this road, you will eventually get there. Certainly there will be obstacles along the way. You could call them failures. But you climb out of the holes and over the broken tree limbs on your path and keep going. These failures are never as significant as your eventual success.

When Tony Bill told me he loved my screenplay and wanted to hire me to write a movie, was this outweighed by 120 rejections I'd had? Not even close. In fact that one victory eclipsed all those failures completely. Blew them right off the historical charts. They were instantly reduced to dues I had already paid and was *proud* to have paid. They became nothing more than an example that might encourage others. They were no longer a negative factor for me.

Do you see? Success and failure are *not* equal. They aren't even in the same reality base. Failures are the potholes and crap littering the road to success. We pick ourselves up, bandage our skinned egos, wipe off our shoes, and keep going. Success unlocks a door into a whole new life in which we are invited to play the game of our dreams. It offers the chance to be in the real world the person you are in your heart. A professional screenwriter.

I was 19 when I knew I wanted to write screenplays more than anything else in the world. I was finally hired to write a movie a few days before my twenty-fifth birthday. That's six years. It was another four years before I sat in a dark screening room looking up at the flickering screen to see my name under the magic words "Written by."

That's ten years altogether. For someone 19, ten years is an unthinkable duration. You expect to be famous in a month. While that's an unrealistic expectation, it is certainly not impossible. I've personally known many new writers who have sold their first, second, or third screenplay for six-figure sums, and continued on to second and third glamorous deals almost immediately. It's okay to fantasize about these possibilities. In fact, it may be necessary to your survival as a screenwriter.

So, while you're struggling through doubt and demoralization, remember:

Work hard. Take chances. Be very, very bold.
The competition is narrowing.
Imagine your movies on the screen.
Don't let rejection stop you.
Keep writing.
Don't set a time limit.
The path you're on leads only to success.

PART TWO

Getting Work

CHAPTER 10

Getting the Most from Your Agent

Early in your relationship with your agent, ideally just prior to signing, set up a get-acquainted lunch meeting. Before the meeting, get your goals organized so that during the meal you can lay them out clearly. Your agent is working for you. He or she needs to know what you want. What is your big-picture career plan? Be prepared to fill him/her in on:

☑ **Where your various projects are now.**

☑ **What you could have ready on short notice.** What you could get to him soon if he shows enthusiasm for it.

☑ **How much money you want or need to make per year.** Ask him if he feels this is a realistic figure. How much does he think you will most likely make the first year?

☑ **The arena you most want to work in.** Features only, television long form, series, books, etc.

☑ **The genres you prefer and are good at.** Mysteries, thrillers, comedies, love stories, epics, etc.

☑ **Whether you are willing to do rewrites.**

☑ **What your long-range goals are.** Producing? Directing? By when?

☑ **Any subjects that you don't want to have anything to do with.** Either because they go against your morals or are just not to your taste. Maybe you'll do thrillers but not slashers, for example.

I always have a list with me of things I want to be sure to cover during lunch. My agent and I both love our business so we don't waste too much time pretending to talk about anything else. Plates of salad and pasta come and go without distracting us from the job at hand.

Here is an abbreviated sketch of a typical first lunch with an agent. Begin with getting him (in this case, my agent Dave) up to speed with your projects that may already be in play or in progress. In my case, I already had a career in progress and had left another agency to go with Dave, so there were things to fill him in on.

DAVE: You want to start or should I?

CYNTHIA: I'll start. Consider me available. I still have one more draft on the Georgia MOW (movie of the week) for CBS which I'll turn in next week. I've put the UFO script aside for the moment because I can't come up with an ending yet that doesn't fall into the *Close Encounters* trap or *The Abyss*. I want to adapt my play that you read, about the two women friends, into a screenplay, but I haven't gotten very far yet.

DAVE (who can eat and listen at the same time): Bring me the latest draft of the play. I think we should start sending it around to a few actresses as it is and see if we can get some interest. Who do you see in it?

CYNTHIA: It's a blonde and a brunette that are opposites. Could be Meg Ryan and Sandra Bullock or younger, Kate Hudson and Neve Campbell.

DAVE: Let me work on that. Try and come up with an ending to the UFO piece. I know somebody who is looking for the next big *X Files*-type sci-fi adventure.

CYNTHIA: Okay. Can we talk about the overall game plan?

DAVE: Sure.

CYNTHIA: I'm doing a book on screenwriting that will pass on my screenwriting class, but it's taken a few months and the money is not much. So I need something in September that can bring in some money pretty quickly.

DAVE: Will you still consider doing some rewrites? Probably no writing credit, but short time frame for the money.

CYNTHIA: Yes. That's perfect. I'm most interested at this point in writing love stories, teenage girl comedies like vintage John Hughes with a current twist. *Pretty in Pink 2003*, that kind of thing. I think there's a vacuum there. Lot's of teen boy flicks, but not much for the girls.

DAVE: I agree. It's an untapped niche right now.

CYNTHIA: I want to do positive, uplifting, life-affirming stories. No "ain't it awful" pictures, and I want to steer clear of movies about prisons, hospitals, divorce, child abuse, and addicts.

DAVE: Fine. I'll always call you first when I find out about a project to see if you're interested in the subject before I go on a major campaign to try to get you the assignment.

CYNTHIA: Great. When I finish the CBS thing and the UFO ending, I'll bring in a list of other ideas and you can strategize pitches.

DAVE (draining his iced tea): Don't worry. We'll keep you busy.

By the end of the lunch meeting, you should each have a list of two or three things to follow up on. At the end of this lunch my list was:

- Get Dave latest copy of the play.
- Finish the final polish of the CBS movie.
- Find an ending to the UFO script.
- Compile a list of possible projects Dave could set up pitches for.

Dave's List:

- Go out and find a quick rewrite job for good money.
- Strategize actresses that could make the play a movie and send it to them.
- Look around for feature assignments Cynthia might be right for.

Telephoning Your Agent

Phone calls are considerably shorter meetings, but the same rules of thumb apply:

• Don't call without a specific purpose. Avoid making "What's happening?" phone calls unless there are specific projects pending that you need to be updated on; even then, don't make these calls too often.

• Jot down all the items you need to talk about so you can cover everything in one call.

• Don't waste time with small talk.

• Don't call your agent to complain about a project or producers unless there is something specific your agent can do about it. An agent is not a best friend, nor is she a therapist. Find another place to deal with your emotional swings about your careening career. Your agent is somebody you call to do business with and to convey and receive good news and bad. No whining.

If your agent knows that every time you call it will be a brief, non-hysterical conversation that will accomplish something, he will get in the habit of returning your calls before others on his list.

If you sit by the telephone, hoping, praying and doing nothing else but waiting for your agent to get you work before your money runs out, you are destined to be very unhappy with him or her.

If you want your agent to be able to guide and promote you into a stellar writing career, you have to provide the raw material. You need to create a continuous flow of scripts, stories, and ideas to pitch.

Your agent's job is to *place* the material that you produce; to *connect* you and your ideas to the right producer who can make them happen; and to *negotiate* the best possible deal when the time comes.

You are the factory; he is the retail outlet. If the factory is not producing the goods, the retailer can't sell them.

CHAPTER 11

The Pitch

There was once a time, legend has it, when all you had to do to be a successful writer was to write well. This is not quite true anymore. At least not in the film industry. A great script just isn't enough. You'll hear people say, "Yes, it's a great script. I love it, but we already have something like it in development." "Tristar has green-lit another project that takes place in Tibet," or "It's just not castable." Whatever the reason, the sample script is often not bought. If the writing is good enough, however, the next question is always, "What other ideas do you have? What do you want to do next?" The object of this inquiry is the possibility of a development deal.

The most common route to a development deal is through the pitch. Today a writer has to be an actor, a barker, a storyteller, a song and dance man, a—pardon the expression—salesman.

Unfortunately, most personality traits that make good writers (listening well, observing quietly, spending long hours alone with a computer) are not necessarily associated with the ability to pitch a story enthusiastically to strangers in a high-pressure situation. But the film business now requires it. I'm not saying that it's a desirable system, but it is the way things are. If you want to work regularly writing and selling screenplays, you had better learn to pitch and to pitch well. Short of being a certified genius with phenomenal luck or a member of Steven Spielberg's immediate family, you're going to have to pitch your ideas.

An overwhelming number of deals in this industry are created in pitch meetings. These might take place in locales like a studio or network executive's office, at one of the trendier watering holes, or from a couple of chaise longues around a producer's pool. In spite of Polo Lounge mythology, most meetings take place in offices, as most executives and producers conduct business in more or less usual ways.

How to Get a Meeting

Once you have an agent, he or she will set up meetings for you; however, this is not the only way to arrange meetings. Once you have written a screenplay that is solid and polished, you will be able to get people to read it. Once a producer or production executive has read it and loves it, he or she may ask if you have any other ideas you'd like to come in and talk about. If they don't suggest it, you can mention that you have some other ideas you'd like to tell them about. With both you and your agent working at it, a meeting is likely to be arranged.

If you can't get a meeting right away with an executive, then set up meetings with development people, story editors, producer's assistants, or anyone who can potentially get your story to someone who can make a deal with you. At the very least this will be good practice in pitching, and it could lead to real employment. Even if these secondary people can't get you in with the executives who can say yes, chances are that within a couple of years (or sooner) they'll *be* the people who can say yes. And they'll already know you.

Another thing you should know about producers' assistants, development people, and story editors is that most of them are trying to move up. And one of the ways for them to get ahead is for them to discover a brilliant new script, story, or writer. If the timing is right, they can "discover" you, and this can be equally beneficial to both your careers.

Dressing for Success

In the movie business, it's not only the actors who have to look the part. Everybody in the business is sensitive to looks and impressions; they're always quietly determining who and what you are by how you come across, physically and verbally. So make sure you're projecting the image that serves you best.

If you want to be seen in the role of successful, confident screenwriter, you might want to make some changes in your personal wardrobe department. It's true that if you are a comedy writer you can be a bit more eccentric. Jeans and T-shirts have been a writer's uniform for a couple of decades now, but they have to be the right jeans and right T-shirts. (Not less cool, say, than The Gap.) Emphasis in Hollywood is still on youth. So if you need to, touch up that gray hair.

Get yourself set up in one outfit that makes you feel like a winner. You have to look like you have money or are at least comfortable with it. In giving you a development deal, they are trusting you with thousands of dollars—and want to feel that it's unlikely you'll run off to Machu Pichu with their money. Your clothes need to be attractive, easy, and comfortable. You should have no attention on your clothes or your appearance. You have to be comfortable sitting and pitching, leaning forward, without worrying about a short skirt riding up. Nothing too sexy. Your main purpose is to have all the attention in the room focused on your story, so minimize distractions.

A brief note on your car. No doubt you have heard about the car culture in Hollywood. Driving a Rolls Silver Cloud will not assure you of big movie deals, but if driving your beat-up old car through the studio gates embarrasses you to the point where you slink into your pitch meeting like the invisible man, hoping no one saw you drive in, it could handicap you. If your car is an eyesore or unsafe even parked at the curb, do yourself a favor and borrow a car for the pitch.

Obviously, looking good won't get you a job, but looking a mess might cost you one. Agents and producers are playing a high-stakes game, and they need to feel confident in you. Don't underestimate the power of looking the part. Do whatever you can to increase your probability of success.

Before the Meeting

Before you ever get to the meeting, there are a few key things that you need to do:

1 Make sure they have read your script. The most important impression you need to make is with your writing. Arrange to have your script read by the person to whom you will be pitching. It is enough for you to have to sell your story to someone in a pitch meeting without also having to convince him that you can write.

2 Do your homework. You must be fully prepared to pitch your story. This means that you know the story backwards and forwards. You may be nervous. Pitching can be frightening. If you have to grope around to recall what happens next, you might lose them. At home, break up your story scene by scene on 3 x 5 cards and lay them out on a storyboard to be sure there are no holes in your structure. If you have to, write the key moments in an abbreviated list on one card you can look over right before you walk into the pitch meeting. Then put it away.

Practice pitching to yourself in a mirror or to friends or family until you are confident that you know the story and can tell it briefly and coherently. Do whatever background research you need so that you can talk about the subject with some authority.

3 Know the producer/executive's credits. Try to find out before the meeting what this person has done before. Give the impression that you've done your homework and want to work with him because you respect his work, not because you're desperate and would take a meeting with anyone in town. If you can't find out ahead of time, once you get to the office, study the walls carefully. Most of these people have framed posters and ads all over the walls, so it's not hard to figure out what they've done. You can use this as an opening remark once the meeting begins. "I loved your remake of *The Scarlet Pimpernel* even better than the Leslie Howard version." But don't lie about having seen something that you didn't see. It can become quickly embarrassing if the conversation continues.

The Pitch Meeting

Sometimes these meetings can be a bit intimidating. One executive, who looked like a direct descendant of Vito Corleone, ushered me into his office, then pushed a hidden button under his desk and the door closed silently behind me. Scary, but you need to forget about everything but the story.

Even more difficult than pitching to a mob type is pitching to a movie star. Some of today's producers and directors are also movie stars. Mel Gibson, Kevin Costner, and Ben Affleck all wear multiple hats. This can be very distracting, but try not to be incapacitated. And keep eye contact, even if the butterflies in your stomach are miniature cupids.

Whatever the setup, don't let it throw you. Here's how it works:

You arrive at the outer office (on time). His assistant tells you he'll be right with you and asks if you'd like something to drink. I usually ask for water in case my mouth goes dry, or in case I need a few extra moments mid-pitch to collect my racing thoughts or to concoct an answer to an unexpected question.

It might well be that the guy has kept you waiting for 10 or 15 minutes. Act as if this is nothing. To them, it *is* nothing. It's normal. It is not personal. But you are finally ushered into the inner office. Who is in the meeting? It can range from just the two of you to five or six and sometimes even more. If you and a producer or team of producers are pitching, maybe with a star or director attached, or both, then your team walks in as a group. And the executive often has a development person, or an assistant who may be taking notes, so the room could be fairly crowded. The smaller the meeting, the better. When several people are present they all may feel the need to put their two cents in, and that's often two cents worth of criticism.

Occasionally the executive's assistant will be a young, intellectual junior exec right out of Yale Drama School or the English Department at Harvard, who is being groomed by the executive. This kind of extra feedback threw me the first time I encountered it. The assistant may bring up some kind of criticism of the story, usually in literary terms whose meaning may elude you. You could be made to feel stupid even if you've recently reread Aristotle's *Poetics*. Be gracious about this. If you haven't the vaguest notion of what she is talking about, you can always say something like "Interesting point. I'll have to take that into consideration." I have to admit I didn't handle the first HEM (Harvard English Major) I encountered at a story meeting well at all. I think I said something like "I'm sorry, I wrote this story passionately out of my heart and you're coming from such an analytical, left-brain place, it just doesn't compute with what I'm trying to do." This, of course, made me sound even stupider than I felt.

Getting back to the meeting, you walk into the inner office and say hello, shaking hands with the executive. (People used to say, "I'm glad to meet you." Now, afraid of not remembering having met someone before, they all say, "Good to see you.") And you quickly glance around the room to size things up. Case the joint.

Seating Strategy

Most executive offices have a large desk with a chair on one side of the room and a couch with one or two armchairs on the other side. You should be able to get an immediate sense of which chair the executive always sits in to hear pitches. Try to put yourself in the best seat to pitch to that chair. Avoid the couch if at all possible. The couch is dangerous territory. Most of these are low, wide, and much too soft. Some are even down-filled, the worst for pitching. When you sink into one of these, before you know it you are semi-reclined and half buried, your voice muffled and your listeners drowsy. Better to pick an uncomfortable, stiff-backed chair. If you have no choice but the couch, sit up straight on the edge for the pitch. You need to be leaning toward your listeners to get the maximum energy into your delivery.

Now everybody's got a seat and it's time for a little small talk. This can be anything from complimenting the exec on one of his movie's weekend grosses to how the Lakers are doing. Or your producer may do an opening preamble and then turn it over to you.

If you're alone in the room with the executive, when she feels there's been enough banter, she'll get down to business. "I hear you have a new project you want to talk about." Or words to that effect. And you're on.

Time

These meetings last a bit less than 30 minutes and are scheduled every half hour. The pitch itself should last 10 to 15 minutes. This leaves time for small talk at the beginning and questions and some discussion at the end.

The Pitch Itself

A good pitch should be very much like telling your best friend about a terrific movie that you saw the night before—and you know your friend won't have a chance to see it. So you try to tell it so she'll feel like she saw the movie. It should be told with plenty of enthusiasm and should elicit the same emotional response in the listener that the movie would. If it's a tear-jerker, there should be a lump in their throats. If it's suspenseful, goose bumps should rise. And if it's a comedy, you'd better tell it in such a way that you get some laughs.

Keep your eye on your audience. And pitch to the one person in the room who can put your project in development. Often a less important person will look much more interested, and it is tempting to play to the audience that is loving it. But you can't afford to ignore the power player. Pretend he or she is the only person in the room and play it straight to that face. If they look glazed over, skip immediately to the next exciting, dramatic plot point. They won't notice the jump. Their mind has already wandered. You've got to get their attention back as soon as possible.

Opening Lines

Always let them know up front, in a sentence, what kind of movie you're pitching. This avoids their spending the first five minutes trying to figure out if it's supposed to be funny or frightening. When and where is this taking place? You need to orient them right away. If you have a great opening pitch line, this is the place to use it.

You can, of course, always use a simple line like "This is an action adventure set in the Mayan ruins of the Yucatan." Or: "This is a wacky comedy about a couple of tennis pros who have triplets." These are clear and to the point even if they don't have the punch of some of the more famous successful pitch lines, like *"High Noon* in outer space" *(Outland);* "*Summer of '42* with cars" *(American Graffiti);* "*Romeo and Juliet* on drugs" *(Panic in Needle Park).*

Some noteworthy ad lines would have made good openings for pitches: "If adventure had a name, it would be Indiana Jones" *(Raiders of the Lost Ark).* "They're young. They're in love. They kill people" *(Bonnie and Clyde).* "What other men called hell, he called home" *(Rambo).*

Try to be original. When word was out that a studio was looking for romantic comedies, they were getting 50 pitches a week that started with the line "It's a modern Tracy-Hepburn movie."

Interruptions

If the executive to whom you're pitching is important, the chances are pretty good that he'll take one or two phone calls during the half hour that he's listening to you. (You may hear him say to his assistant as you all go in, "Hold everyone except Howard or David." Often they have a picture shooting and if there's a crisis on location, they have to be reachable.) If a phone call interrupts your pitch, don't let it throw you. Hold that thought exactly where you left off. When he's finished with the call, he'll come back saying, "I'm sorry about that." Don't waste more time by getting into a conversation like "Hey, that's okay. I understand." No. Just go right on exactly where you left off. Don't lose one single ounce of energy or focus or conviction.

If you go in with one or two producers as a team, they may—during the pitch—interrupt you to add or emphasize something. Never make it look like this is annoying or distracting to you. I always force myself to smile and nod while they are doing this. Act as if it's adding to the positive energy of the pitch. Use it. Build on it. Make it work to your advantage.

Occasionally the executive will interrupt you to ask a question or to ask you to clarify a point. Answer him, but *do not lose your thread.*

If You Leave Out Something Really Important

It happens. Even if you've practically memorized your pitch. It's okay. Really. Do not say "Oh, no. I forgot to put in the part where . . ." No. What you gracefully say is, as if you planned it exactly this way, "What you also need to know is that three days earlier Jane hid a bottle of lye in the footlocker . . ." Like that. Smooth as you can. If you act as if you planned it this way, it turns out as well as if you actually did.

Extra Ammunition

Once in a while it works to bring in a little something extra. If it's a true story, sometimes documentation, photos, or news clippings can be useful. Here are a couple of examples of props in pitches that helped to sell them in the room:

I pitched a past-life murder drama based on a real case. We had the rights to an intriguing case of a hypno-therapist. A woman had remembered under hypnosis being murdered in 1927—having just heard on the radio that Lindbergh had landed after his history-making trans-Atlantic flight. And she also remembered her first name in that life, the dress and shoes she was wearing, and that her body was dumped over Niagara Falls afterwards. We had the tapes of the session under hypnosis, but what sold this story was the moment we pulled out a copy of the front page of the Buffalo (New York) newspaper for that day in 1927. It was found by the therapist while visiting in upstate New York. He looked it up in the library microfilm archives on a whim. The front page was shared by Lindbergh's landing—and the body of a murdered woman found below Niagara Falls. This physical proof of an outrageous tale actually elicited a gasp in the room at the end of the pitch. (Of course, we saved the punch line for the end.) It meant a thriller past-life drama could include the heading: Based on a True Story. They bought it on the spot. (The TV movie was called *Search for Grace* and starred Lisa Hartman Black and Ken Wahl.)

While researching a pitch for a project on the Civil Rights Movement and the march from Selma to Montgomery, I found at the library an audio recording of the actual march. You could hear feet walking, cars speeding by, and the people singing as they marched, the great songs of the Movement. It made the event so real and immediate that I copied the recording onto a cassette tape to play for my producer. He loved it so much he brought it into the pitch meeting and played it on a small tape-recorder in the background while I told the story. When I got to the dramatic peaks, he would turn up the volume to heighten the drama. About two-thirds of the way through the pitch, the executive stopped me and said, "I have to tell you I love this story, I'm going to buy this, but I can't believe you're doing this. Now go ahead and tell me the rest." I did, and she did. Sometimes these things help.

Be sure you consider the prop or visual aid from the producer's point of view. If you're telling a children's story along the lines of *The Velveteen Rabbit* and bring in a stuffed animal, it could push it too far over the top and blow the pitch. You may be pitching to a guy who *hates* stuffed animals; he could relate to the story as a children's film, but the toy turns him off. Get the idea? Consider any such presentation aid before you bring a lot of stuff into the pitch. It could help, but it could backfire. Use your own best judgment.

Written Notes

Should you bring a written outline to help you remember your pitch? No. Practice until you can do it from memory. Do not use a cheat sheet for pitching. You need your attention to be 100% on the story, directed 100% to the listener.

But "Should you have written pitch pages with you?" is another question. Rarely does the person you are pitching to have the ability to buy your project on the spot. Normally these executives listen to pitches all week and bring their two or three favorites into the weekly staff meeting, where they go around the table and pitch the two or three best pitches they've heard that week to the rest of the team and the top execs.

Let's say you pitched your story to Guy on Friday afternoon. The staff meeting is Tuesday, and he is trying to narrow his five favorite pitches down to two. And yours was great, but kind of complicated and he's not sure he can retell it without messing up the plot. He might pick his second choice and drop yours just to save himself the embarrassment of blowing it. But, if at the end of your pitch meeting, he said, "Do you have any pages to leave with me?" And you pulled out a clear, concise three-page beat sheet and handed it to him, enabling him to able to brush up on your story and tell it well. Days later, it could improve your odds.

The Writers Guild does not sanction this, as it is technically writing without compensation, but it is easy to see how a beat sheet or cheat sheet could help your career. So I do it. Also, if you had a great newspaper article, photo, or paper prop that put it over in the pitching room, leave that behind as well, if it is requested. Make sure you have made copies ahead. Never have just one copy of any of these props. You won't get it back, and you may need to pitch again.

The more you understand about what goes on behind closed doors at the studios and how business is done, the better you can design your own strategies for succeeding in the Hollywood studio arena.

When Disaster Strikes

At the other end of the spectrum are those pitches where you know as soon as you begin that the movie is never going to happen. One sentence into the pitch, the executive says, "Oh, no. I've got something like this already in development. But go ahead. Tell it to me anyway." Stop right here. Put the brakes on. Do not proceed with your planned pitch. You know there's no way he's going to develop two similar scripts, and now you're going to give him all your best ideas which could end up in his similar project? (Can't you just imagine him saying months later, after you see your bits in his movie, "I *told* you I already had a project just like it.")

Try to extricate yourself gracefully with something like, "No, no. I don't want to waste your time if you've already got a similar project. What about an action adventure set in Tanzania?" Slide right into a casual pitch of a back-up project if you've got one. You should always have a couple of back-burner ideas perking for moments like this. Be flexible. You can always pitch your main project somewhere else. Just because he already has one like it is no guarantee that his will be shot—or that there's not room for another similar movie. Pitch yours to the studio across the street. Stay sharp. Work on your ability to think fast on your feet and not be thrown, no matter what they throw at you.

Another example of a worst-case pitching scenario: As I walked into an executive's office at a major motion picture studio, the executive said to his assistant, "Hold all calls unless it's the hospital." Then he turned to us apologetically and explained that his wife was in surgery. Well, forget it. Every time the phone in the outer office rang, he turned white, waiting to see if it was the hospital. I don't think he heard one word of the story. His glazed look never wavered. If something like this happens, cut your losses and get out as simply and quickly as you can. This is just one of the eleven pitches that don't lead to a job. But you're one step closer to the twelfth.

The Power of "Yes" – and No Power

After a pitch, there may be some small talk. Maybe a few questions. Don't be surprised if people don't let on whether they liked it or not. It doesn't necessarily mean that they don't. There is a good reason for this mysteriousness. In almost every case, the person you are pitching to doesn't have the power to say yes without getting the approval of someone higher up the studio or network ladder. The people who can say yes rarely meet with writers and producers directly. They have development people to do that for them.

Once you have made your pitch to the executive, if he likes it, he then has to go to his boss and pitch it to him. Be sure that you pitch it clearly and enthusiastically so it can be repeated by someone else who has been infected by your excitement.

The executives who listen to pitches all day really want you to believe that they have the power to say yes. If they were to show their excitement in a meeting, they'd have to come back, tails between their legs, if they get a "no" from their higher-ups. They'd have to admit that they really didn't have the power to make a deal. So keeping a poker face is a matter of protecting their status.

I must add that there are, thankfully, exceptions to this. There are several executives in town who are openly enthusiastic if they like something, and are quite candid about having to convince their bosses.

Though the executives for the most part don't have the power to say yes, they all have the power to say no. This is unfortunate, but true. If they don't like the pitch or if it is too close to something else that they are developing, they can pass on a project without further discussion.

Never Tell Everything You Know in a Pitch

The people at your meeting will almost always want to talk about it afterwards. This usually involves asking for more details or background on one point or another. If you have already told them everything you know in the pitch, you'll have to punt at the end and it will leave things on a weaker note. Save something for this inevitability.

Never Tell Every Scene

When you pitch a story it should flow quickly from major story point to major story point. If you start out describing every shot and where the camera is, they're going to start worrying that this story may take two hours to pitch.

Do Not Pitch the Story to Anyone Else
Until You Have an Answer

As I've already pointed out, word gets around unbelievably fast in this town. If you pitch the same story again before you've gotten a response, you are implying that you don't believe the first pitch is going to sell it. This is a negative attitude. Act like you believe that everyone you pitch to is going to love your story and buy it. Be patient. Usually they will let you know within a week or two. Sometimes they take longer. Hollywood is famous for the "slow no." Work on other stories while you wait.

If You Really Can't Pitch to Save Your Life

If you are really terrible at pitching—and there are some wonderful and successful writers who are truly awful at it—it's not the end of the world. There are a few viable alternatives. The best is to find a dynamic producer who is terrific at pitching and go in to pitch together. You can work out the story in detail ahead of time and after an opening sentence or two, just say, "Larry's really better at this, so he's going to tell you my story." Always do what works best for you.

A Sample Pitch

For your pitch, pick a couple of scenes to tell in detail so that they can visualize them. In this case, I chose an opening with a strong hook, and then the last two scenes. The rest you can sketch in, making sure it is clear that you've already worked the whole story out:

The Pitch

It's called *Jane Doe* and it's a suspense thriller about a woman who was found buried alive in a shallow grave who has no memory of what happened to her or who she is.

The movie opens on a field at dusk. Autumn. Mists on the ground. A boy walks home with his dog. The dog starts sniffing around in the dead leaves. The boy calls him, but the dog is digging now. Finally the boy has to come back for him, but as he bends down to grab the dog's collar, he sees a *hand* sticking out of the dirt.

BAM! Police cars. Red lights flashing, surrounding the area. Flash of police cameras. A detective is in charge as they carefully unearth the nude body of a woman from the shallow grave, careful not to damage any evidence. She is the fourth victim of a serial killer who has been terrorizing the area. Suddenly somebody yells, "I've got a *pulse* here!"

BAM! In the ambulance, siren screaming, racing to the hospital. They get her into the ER, and she pulls through. But when she wakes up in the hospital she has no memory of anything. It's as if the moment she was being strangled she was so sure that it was the end, that her mind checked out.

Four interwoven storylines follow:

The Detective Story: The police trying to find the killer before he strikes again. Our detective determined to break through Jane's wall of amnesia, willing to use any methods to jolt her into remembering, including taking Jane back to look into her own grave.

The Psychological Story: A caring woman psychologist works with Jane, using hypnosis. Jane has nightmares with images that piece together the attack, but not the killer's face. The psychologist tries to protect Jane from the detective.

The Family Story: Jane's mother trying to find her. The police try to determine if she is really who she claims to be. A man shows up claiming to be her husband. Is he? Or is he the killer trying to get to her?

The Killer's Story: The serial murderer sees it on the news and makes plans to finish Jane before she can remember and identify him.

All four stories come together at the climax of the movie. The police have brought the killer in for a lineup, but don't have enough to hold him if Jane doesn't identify him. She looks at each face, but doesn't remember. The police have to let him go, and they send Jane back to the hospital. But as she crosses the parking lot, her flashbacks intensify, triggered by having seen him, and she finally remembers the killer! At that moment she looks up and he is right in front of her!

He chases her to the car. She manages to get inside but drops the keys under the seat. Just as she gets them, his arm comes through the window grabbing her hair. She gets the car started. He disappears for a moment, then reappears suddenly with a hammer, smashes the windshield, jumps on the hood of the car, grabs the steering wheel. The car careens out of control, until he loses his grip and falls under the wheels. Jane pulls the car over, sobbing. The detective appears telling her she's okay. It's over.

When the detective walks her back through the hospital lobby, Jane's mother is there waiting and Jane sees her and says, "Mom?" And they are crying in each other's arms as we FADE OUT.

[END OF PITCH]

This pitch took about ten minutes and was almost verbatim as written above. The executive bought the project on the spot, and it became a CBS movie staring Karen Valentine, William Devane, and Eva Marie Saint. It was nominated for the Edgar Allan Poe Award.

Pitching has become a necessary tool for communicating the concept of a movie in a kind of shorthand. It might seem secondary to the writer's craft, and it *is* secondary, but it's a skill you should develop in order to have every possible advantage you can as you scale the walls of Fortress Hollywood.

CHAPTER 12

Occupational Hazards and Fringe Benefits

If only one out of every 50 screenplays owned by a studio gets filmed, what happens to the rest of them? Good question. There are a lot of ways in which films don't get made. But when they do get as far as being shot, there are lots of perks to make up for the previous misses. Below are some of the things that can go wrong—and right.

The Hazards

Turnaround

This is just a dignified word for a screenplay being put on the shelf. Your script was developed for a studio which then decides, for any number of reasons, that it won't be shot. The script then goes into "turnaround," which means it becomes available to be purchased from the first studio by another producer or studio. Generally the price is enough to reimburse the original studio that developed the screenplay for its initial investment.

Occasionally, a screenplay that was in turnaround for one studio is bought by another, and made. It does happen, just not often.

The two best ways to improve the odds of your film getting made are:

• Write one or two central roles—showy roles that could conceivably get nominated for awards. (See Chapter 4.)

• Don't write an ending that is so depressing and low-energy that the script reader is contemplating suicide by the last page. Most movies that

Hollywood shoots have upbeat endings. I'm not trying to restrict your creativity, just letting you know what the market is. Even the "heaviest" studio films like *Schindler's List* and *Saving Private Ryan* have upbeat endings. Did Schindler save the people on the list? Was Private Ryan saved? You bet.

What Happens When Studios Change Regimes?

Every few years, most movie and television studios undergo a large turnover at the executive level. A new head will come in and bring in a whole new top-level staff, retaining only a handful of the former executives. The turnover rate for company presidents is extremely high. Since it may take from six months to a year to develop a screenplay through several drafts, and even longer to get a green light and a shoot date, it is quite common for studio heads to change in the middle of screenplay deals.

When this occurs, it is a crapshoot whether your development deal will be totally dropped, be nominally completed and then dropped, or survive. The new group doesn't want to put energy into high-visibility projects for which the former regime will take credit. They want all new projects. *Their* projects. I have been in several situations where a screenplay has been given a film order (green light) only to have an executive turnover put it on the shelf. Green lights can turn to red. Don't break open the champagne until the first day of principal photography.

Being Beaten to the Punch

Sometimes you are in the middle of a development deal and a competing studio will announce they are shooting something very similar. Or worse, they will release a movie too close to yours for comfort.

Let's pause here for a little story, one I call:

Crapping Out in the Big Casino

In the fall of 1998 I got a terrific development deal to write a feature film for Dreamworks, based on a novel they had bought the rights to. They had many screenwriters to choose from, but based on one of my feature screenplays they had read, and a get-to-know-you meeting, they chose me. I was thrilled.

Our story meetings took place at Amblin, a fabulous Santa Fe-style hacienda, tucked away in a corner of the Universal Studios lot. The original nine-foot Tyrannosaurus Rex from *Jurassic Park* stands on the coffee table. After our first meetings they were sending me to Maine to do the research. The story involved a Maine lobster fisherman as the romantic lead. So the research trip was arranged.

To put this in perspective, for a TV movie research trip, I would make all the arrangements, park in the airport economy lot, and afterwards bill the company for my expenses and they'd reimburse me. Dreamworks, however, has its own travel agent in-house. They had a driver (in a uniform with a limo) pick me up at my house and drop me at my gate—where a first-class plane ticket was waiting for me. And they arranged a place for me to stay in Portland, Maine. The exact conversation went like this:

DREAMWORKS TRAVEL AGENT: I found a fabulous place for you to stay.

CYNTHIA: For future reference, I'll be glad to stay any place that has the word "fabulous" in front of it.

It was a fabulous place: "The Danforth," an 1854 mansion converted into an elegant hotel. My room had an antique writing desk, fireplace, harbor view, and breakfast in bed as part of the deal. But after one night, it was clear to me that I needed to be out in the little fishing villages, not in a city, so I started at the southernmost tip of the Maine coast and worked my way "down east" as they say, getting almost as far as Bar Harbor.

The time I spent with a by-God real lobster man, poking around his boat, the docks, traps, lobsters, barrels of bait, asking dozens of questions, was pure gold. I got the guys—the accent, attitude, and attire. Picture orange rubber overalls, plaid flannel shirts, and hats with earflaps up, huge rubber boots. He asked, "Do you think Mel Gibson would wear an Elmer Fudd hat?" Dry humor. The typical Maine joke is: "Have you lived in Maine all your life?" "Not yet."

I came home loaded with great material and went to work. A few weeks later disaster struck.

Our project was a dramatic love story set in Maine about a guy who works on boats, falls in love, the lovers end apart, and the audience cries. On Valentine's Day weekend, *Message in Bottle* opened—a dramatic love story shot in Maine about a guy who works on boats, and ditto the rest of that sentence. Its second weekend, it tanked. And three days later I was out of a deal. If the public doesn't want to see that movie with Kevin Costner in it, well, it probably doesn't want to see that movie, period.

And that was the end of the Dreamworks dream work. I was no longer "working for Steve Spielberg," as my kids liked to put it. I was paid to go away and write nothing. The amount of the payoff was an extremely round number that was hard to turn down. (How round, exactly, I am not allowed to say.) Did the money make me feel better? A little.

The moral to the story is, one more time, in unison: It's a crapshoot. Sometimes when it looks like it's coming up seven, at the last possible moment, the winning dice flop over into craps. Sometimes losers can also roll over, however. And then it's Cinderella time. Be fearless. And don't stop rolling those dice.

If Your Script Turns Into a Nightmare

If everything goes wrong and your script is shelved, you can sometimes get the rights to your script back again. The WGA has a stipulation that if it is an original screenplay based on no outside material, and is shelved, the rights may revert to you after several years. At the moment, it's seven, but this could change. Check with the WGA to see current status if and when you need this information.

If you can't wait seven years, and your beloved script is languishing on the shelf in turnaround, you may be able to buy it back if you can afford to. One of my former students sold a screenplay of his to a smaller, but well-known studio. It was a psychological thriller/mystery along the lines of *Psycho.* When he began doing revisions for pay, he realized that the studio's intention was to turn his script, which he cared about deeply, into a slasher exploitation film. With each draft he became progressively more depressed about it and finally realized that he couldn't do it anymore and wanted his original screenplay back.

He borrowed enough money and repaid everything they had paid him; they gave him back the rights to the script. They didn't have to do this, but they agreed to. I admire this young writer for having the passion and ability to do this, but I wouldn't have advised him to spend all of this time and energy. My advice would have been to let it go and move on to the next script. When you have only written a handful of them, each script carries a lot of weight. So keep writing. Nothing helps your perspective as much as having written a lot of screenplays and knowing you will write a lot more. It eases the pain of individual disappointments.

Fringe Benefits

Shooting Bonuses

Feature screenplay deals always include a shooting bonus, which your agent will negotiate into your contract up front. Usually the bonus amounts to more than you are being paid to write the script itself in a development deal. A typical shooting bonus on a $150,000 script sale, for instance, might easily be $250,000.

When do you get the bonus check? Your contract may say that the bonus is due to you on the "first day of principal photography," which means the first day of shooting with actors, as opposed to second-unit photography, which could be shot months sooner to capture a snowstorm or some other seasonal shot. Actually, they usually pay you half the bonus at the start of the shoot, and hold the other half until the WGA determines the writing credits.

Most contracts say that the bonus is yours "if you get sole screenplay credit." If credit is shared, ordinarily you get only half the money. They won't give you the rest of the bonus until the picture wraps, even if there was never another writer on the project. (It gives them a legal reason to hang onto your money a little longer. Even if it's a lame one: "What if we have to hire someone to polish on location?")

Occasionally, as in the case of *Jaws*, a screenplay will be substantially rewritten during the shoot, and the new writer (in this case, Carl Gottleib) will earn co-screenplay credit. So you can usually expect to get the second half of your shooting bonus within four weeks after the end of shooting.

Residuals

Above and beyond the payment for the script's initial purchase, this money is a royalty for running it on television. Whenever a movie, TV movie, or series episode is aired on television, the screenwriter receives a residual. (You don't get a residual the first time a program is aired that was written for TV, but for all other reruns you do.)

The amount of these residuals varies, based on a complex formula involving the number of writers credited, how much they were originally paid, how many times it has been run, and whether it is prime time, daytime or late night, network, cable or syndicated, U.S. or foreign television. You get the idea. It's complicated. You also get residuals for video and DVD sales.

The Writers Guild keeps track of all programming broadcast on television, bills the appropriate companies for you, collects the checks, and forwards them directly to you. You do not pay an agent's commission on residual money.

Residuals are a key reason that successful TV series writers are the wealthiest writers in town. The highest residuals are earned for series that, after several seasons on network, are sold into syndication and rerun for years, bringing in many times more money than the original episode scripts.

Points

This term refers to additional income that can be made as a result of box-office success. Under the points system, a certain percentage (or points) of the net profits that the film earns, after overhead and expenses have been deducted, are theoretically divided among those with points. Most writers' deals include at least a couple of "points."

You have probably heard that a writer will never see any money from points. Hollywood has become famous for "creative bookkeeping" in this area, or more accurately, it has a system for calculating a movie's expenses that virtually eliminates any possibility of having to pay out money on profit percentage points.

Even so, you should have this clause included as part of your contract. Generally, an original screenplay with only one writer might get 5 points. An adaptation or shared credit may get 2½ points. It is also necessary to stipulate that the definition of profits for the writer be the same as for the producer. In other words, you don't want everyone taking his piece of the pie before your share is calculated.

Keith A. Walker wrote the original screenplay of *Free Willy*. It was so successful that it broke $100 million, spawned two sequels and a Saturday morning TV show, and somehow never made a dime of profit. We could fill a chapter with examples just like it.

Every once in a thousand years, a picture will be made on such a shoestring budget and go over the top with such monumental numbers that the point holders have to be paid something. An example of such a film is *American Graffiti*, which was made for a budget of less than $1 million. The cost of publicity, prints, and studio overhead brought the figure up to $1,275,000. The film made $117 million. It is one of the biggest profit margins a studio has ever earned on a small investment, so everyone involved who had points made money. I suspect this was also because George Lucas was a decent and honorable guy. Like I said, once every thousand years . . .

The moral to these stories is simple. If you are well informed and plan ahead, you can minimize the occupational hazards and increase the likelihood of things going your way. In contract negotiations, get as much money up front as possible. Don't trade off a single dollar now for the promise of profit down the road. That road is a dead end. The fringe benefits of a screenwriting career may be a long time coming, but they are worth waiting for.

CHAPTER 13

Writing for Television

Writing for the big screen is a scriptwriter's holy grail. So it is not surprising that writing for television is thought of as a fallback position for many aspiring scriptwriters. Feature writing pays more and may offer greater artistic freedom and classier trappings.

But in practical terms, television is where most of the work is.

If You'd Rather Be Working Than Waiting

There is a tremendous continual demand for scripts (also known as "product") in the television market. So there is a lot more buying for this medium than at feature film studios. In addition to the three television networks, there are also local, syndicated, public, and cable stations on the air 24 hours a day, every day.

Like many screenwriters, I started out writing only scripts for "real movies." After my deal writing *Love Out of Season* for Tony Bill and MGM, I went on immediately to feature film development deals at 20th Century Fox, Warner Brothers, and Universal Studios. After three years, I had been through six of these deals with nothing to show for it but an income and a tall stack of pages sitting on the shelves. I then decided to accept the offer of a TV movie rewrite.

This was in 1980. The project (at CBS) was called *Leave 'Em Laughing*. It was a "page one rewrite," which means they threw out all of the first script and I wrote a completely new one—but for rewrite (less) money.

When the script was finished, to my delight, it was immediately given a green light and my career finally reached stage two. They were making my movie.

Leave 'Em Laughing was a true story of Jack Thum, a small-time birthday party clown, a lovable old guy in Chicago who had raised 37 foster kids and was dying of lung cancer. It was one of those roles that smells like an Emmy Award for an actor; funny and tragic with a handful of big moments in which a performance can shine.

Half a dozen beloved older comedians, most of whom "didn't do TV movies," came after the part. They all wanted to play this guy. CBS chose Mickey Rooney, backed up by a supporting cast of greatly talented actors: Anne Jackson, Red Buttons, William Windom, Alan Garfield, and Elisha Cook Jr. Jackie Cooper directed. Julian Fowles produced. It was a dream come true.

The first day of shooting, I walked onto the soundstage to find the Thum apartment. Every detail was exactly as I had described it in my script, down to the family snapshots tacked to the kitchen bulletin board. It was one of the emotional high points of my entire career.

I was on the set every day of the shoot. I saw all the dailies and every rough cut as the film emerged. And I got tremendous satisfaction from knowing, as I silently watched the dozens of people in the cast and crew doing their jobs, that none of them would be there working if it weren't for me. If the script hadn't been good, the movie wouldn't have been made. I felt like George Bailey in *It's a Wonderful Life*.

You need to relish these moments, because the chances are no one else will acknowledge that you are the source of all the action. Without the script, there is nothing.

I was nominated for the Humanitas Award for *Leave 'Em Laughing*, for "humanizing achievement in television," along with the first writer, with whom I shared the credit. The first writer almost always gets at least half the screenplay or teleplay credit, even if every word is changed. In this case, the story itself, which was true, was essentially the same. (See Chapter 15 for more on credits and arbitration.)

It shouldn't be surprising that on the heels of this experience, I went on to accept a second and a third TV movie offer almost immediately. In the last few years I have written on assignment over 50 TV movie scripts, 25 of which have been filmed and aired nationally on network or cable television.

Original Movies for Television

These used to be called "Movies of the Week" or MOWs for short. In the industry we call it "writing long-form" television. As of this writing, the market has changed dramatically in the last few years. The market for television movies used to be so small you could count them on the fingers of one hand: ABC, CBS, NBC, HBO, and Showtime were the only outlets. Now two things have happened. The three networks have cut way back on producing TV movies. This is cyclical and will doubtless change again. Network TV movies at the moment have been largely replaced by series and "Reality TV" (i.e., *Survivor, Who Wants to Be a Millionaire*, etc.).

Fortunately, this has coincided with a blossoming of peripheral markets. The companies (networks, stations, etc.) making original movies for television now include not only those mentioned above but also Disney Channel, Fox, Fox Family, Lifetime, MTV, Nickelodeon, Oxygen, TBS, TNT, UPN, USA, VH1, WB. More movies than ever are being made for television markets. The work is there.

Researching TV Movie Markets

While there is an abundance of markets, each is unique in its style, vision, and audience. A script perfect for Lifetime, for example, would have no place at TBS, whose motto is "Movies for guys who like movies." An agent can help you place your TV movie project with the right network, but you need to do your homework as well.

Reading. Study *TV Guide* magazine or the TV supplement in your local paper. (If you're serious about this, you should subscribe to *TV Guide* and read each issue carefully.) Look for which companies have regular movie nights on their schedule. CBS Sunday Night Movie, for example. Then make a note of what kind of movies they are making. Are they looking to hang onto their lead-in *Touched by an Angel* audience, for example? It also helps to note each station's hit series, as it is likely that they will be looking for TV movies for their stars to do during hiatus. Networks have favorites. If you're pitching to CBS, it wouldn't be a bad idea to tailor your project as a vehicle for Roma Downey or Jane Seymour. By studying *TV Guide*, you can learn a lot about the market.

Internet. All of the networks and cable channels listed above have websites. A website can tell you a lot about what the audience is for each station. Are they looking for a young, hip audience like MTV? Family or young viewers like Nickelodeon or Disney? Or are they targeting only women (Lifetime) or men (TBS)? A website can tell you in ten minutes what it might take you much longer to figure out any other way. It also gives you a clear list of what movies they are making and buying. On many of these websites you can click on "Original Movies" and it'll practically do your homework for you.

Watching TV. Obviously, you need to study the movies themselves on TV. I have found that it's not helpful in terms of inspiring you to write great quality TV movies, but it is helpful to study them to develop a broader knowledge about the state and size of the field. How much are they spending on locations, action, actors? How much sexual content, violence, and adult language are they using? Do they have commercials on this channel? How often? Do they run a full two-hour movie (HBO), or is it 90 minutes plus commercials in a two-hour slot (networks)?

The Ratio of TV to Film Production

Think about these odds. My score for feature films: zero filmed out of more than a dozen sold. My television score: 25 filmed out of over 50 sold, or one out of two. Obviously, the odds are much better in TV that a sold script will be shot.

My personal score is a bit higher than average. Generally networks develop about five movie scripts for every one they shoot, while movie studios develop more than 50 scripts for every one they shoot! These numbers vary depending on the studio and the current regime. My agent tells me that it's not unusual for a major studio to develop 100 screenplays for every one they shoot.

In the average year, between the big studios and the independents, approximately 200 feature films are made and released in this country. This number represents movies that fall under the auspices of the Writers Guild, which means not the low, low-budget non-union films. In comparison, the TV networks and cable channels make approximately 90 movies a year. If miniseries and movies for cable and syndication are added, it comes to close to 200, nearly equaling the feature-film market. This sounds comparable—until you remember that this represents all of the big-screen feature films, but only a small percentage of all the kinds of television programming that employ screenwriters.

Format and Structure for TV Movies

When you develop a movie for television for a network in a development deal, you write the script in seven acts. Each act break is structured to be a cliffhanger so that audiences won't leave during the commercial. Act 1 is the longest at around 20 minutes/pages. The other acts are of equal lengths, around 10 to 15 pages each.

Otherwise the format is exactly the same as for feature film screenplays. When breaking into the field, I strongly recommend that you do not break your scripts down into television's seven-act structure. They want to see a feature film script as a sample. The ticket to get through the door in this arena is the same as your entrée into feature films: a great, spec feature film script.

Difference in Money Between Feature Films and TV Movies

For new writers, the difference in the up-front development money for TV movies and feature films is not particularly significant. A television writer with one or two credits might easily make $60,000 for writing a television movie for a network. (WGA minimum is around $59,000.) In comparison, I have had a lot of students who had a first feature assignment to develop a screenplay earn around $50,000. (WGA minimums are $48,000 for low-budget features, $91,000 for high-budget.)

The significant difference in pay comes when they shoot the film. The bonus on your $50,000 TV movie script might be in the neighborhood of $10,000. If they shoot your feature film, the bonus is more likely to be in the $100,000 range. Clearly, it's more of a gamble to do a feature, but it's seductive. Would you rather take a 1 in 5 chance on getting $10,000? Or a 1 in 50 (or 1 in 100) chance on $100,000?

There is a tug of war between the alluring promise of big bucks and status you might get by working in features versus the alternate satisfaction you'd get in seeing your television movies actually made. So far, I have never had a $100,000 bonus check in my hand. But over 600 million people have sat for two hours watching my stories and hearing my words on television, and there is tremendous satisfaction in that.

Crossing Back and Forth Between Movies and TV

Trying to break into feature films via television writing is not a practical or productive route. That second-rate stigma can turn into a downright prejudice against TV writers. When he can't think of any other excuse not to like it, it's very easy for a producer or executive to read your movie script or hear your pitch and without really paying attention to the work, say, "It's too much like television." I have known many writers who have run into this problem.

The only genre that seems exempt from this prejudgment is comedy. Many successful TV comedy writers from Mel Brooks to James L. Brooks (*Terms of Endearment* and *As Good As It Gets*) have gone on to brilliant movie careers. Even Steve Martin started out writing for the *Smothers Brothers Show*.

The easy crossover only happens from a position of success. Obviously, success makes it very easy to go from features to television without damaging the writer's career, as evidenced by Aaron Sorkin *(The West Wing)* and many others.

Timing in TV Scriptwriting

While following the basic three-act structure like feature films, television movies are written in seven acts, each of which climaxes in something of a cliffhanger to ensure that the audience won't turn the channel during the ensuing commercial. Like feature scripts, TV scripts shoot about one minute of film for each page of script. The complete TV movie script should be approximately 105 pages long. Because of commercials, it is slightly shorter than a feature screenplay.

The time allotted to a writer to create TV and feature scripts varies, although the end result is the same length. The networks usually give a writer six to eight weeks to write the first draft of a TV movie. A movie studio would give closer to 12 to 16 weeks to write a screenplay, sometimes longer. Things always happen faster in television.

How to Get Television Writing Assignments

Television networks like to supervise closely the writing of scripts that they will eventually film. They rarely buy MOW scripts written on spec—in fact, I know of only a handful of instances in which a spec script became a TV movie. Your entry into writing TV movies is absolutely the same as for features: a great feature spec script.

Here are some of the steps you can take to drum up TV writing jobs.

First, think of two or three strong or exciting movie ideas that don't require any rights that you don't have. Tell your agent these ideas and ask him to find you a producer or network executive who he feels might respond to these stories. He should help you make a master plan and send your sample spec script to these people ahead of the meetings.

Then, go in and pitch to the television people, just as you would for feature films.

Writing for a Series

If your goal is to write for a TV series, study the field by watching the shows that interest you. Learn all you can about the characters, background, style, and most important, about the tastes of the people making the show. Most series are primarily staff-written, but a few episodes each season are usually left open to be written by non-staff writers.

Do not write a sample episode script of the show you are trying for. If you really want to write a *Will and Grace* episode, for example, don't have your agent submit a spec *Will and Grace* to the show's producer. The people who work on the show know it so well that they will tend to pick apart your spec script, finding faults that they wouldn't see in another show's script. In addition, since they spend their whole lives coming up with *Will and Grace* ideas, the chances are fairly good that whatever story you come up with, they have already thought of. They may even be in the process of developing that show. They also don't want to run the risk of a spec writer hollering "Thief!" if the next season includes an episode that is close to that sample script.

So if you want to write *Will and Grace,* write a brilliant spec script of a series with the same style of comedy. *Just Shoot Me,* for example. Be careful not to submit sample scripts of TV series no longer on the air, or scripts that are dated by using characters that have been dropped. This means you may have to write new series sample scripts every few months until you begin getting those assignments.

Pilots

Many a naïve new writer thinks up a great idea for a series, figures out who the characters are, makes up a dozen episode stories, and even writes the pilot episode on spec. This hopeful writer is often someone who works in a stock brokerage firm who sees how funny and fast-paced life in his office is and how the people around him could be exaggerated a bit to make them hilarious. Or a dentist's office, travel agency, realty company, etc.

Unfortunately, this is almost a complete waste of time. The people the networks hire to develop pilots and new series are exclusively those who have already proven themselves. There are only two paths you can take to get to "Series Created by You" status.

Path #1

• Write spec series-episode scripts until you get an episode assignment on a show.

• With a series credit or two or more, then have your agent get you on the staff of a show.

• After a few pilots or short-lived series, get on the staff of a hit show.

• Pitch a pilot idea to a network or cable channel that they are convinced to buy.

Path #2

• Write a feature film that is a huge hit and gets you an Oscar nomination.

• On the heels of that glorious victory, pitch a series idea to TV.

This is how Aaron Sorkin got to create *The West Wing.* First he wrote a great play called *A Few Good Men,* then wrote the screenplay of the play, which became a greatly acclaimed film, etc. Get the picture?

Which Path to Take: TV or Feature Films?

The risks and payoffs are high in both features and television. You will do the best work and reap the greatest rewards if you write what you personally care about most. If you never watch television or don't like television, don't try to write it.

On the other hand, if you're a series fanatic and have seen every episode of *Friends* or *Seinfeld* and regularly turn down any dinner date on Wednesday night, no matter how good the restaurant, so you won't miss *The West Wing*, then television writing may be the perfect career for you.

CHAPTER 14

Story Meetings

There is an old saying among screenwriters that executives always want to take one of three things out of a script. The heart, the brain, or the spine. Here are some tips for surviving story meetings with your script anatomically intact.

The Preliminary Story Meeting

This is the executive's and producer's opportunity to "shape" the piece before it is written. You tell them what you intend to do in the screenplay, and they will let you know which of your ideas they like and which they don't like. They may criticize the very things you love the most—the reasons why you took the job in the first place. Or they may make suggestions that throw the story off balance, out of focus, or off the track entirely. They may suggest that you tailor a role to attract a certain kind of actor—who you feel is completely wrong.

The best thing you can do after these meetings is to use the suggestions that you honestly feel will make the screenplay better. Forget the rest. Don't tell them this is what you are planning to do. Just thank them for their input, tell them you felt the meeting was helpful, and go home and write the best screenplay you possibly can.

"What?" you may ask. "Deliberately disobey an order from the person who is paying me all that money?" Well, I look at it this way: This is the only chance you'll ever get to do the story your way. If you compromise it, in your own judgment, before it is even written, you are in for a long, depressing writing experience.

The meeting was about an idea, a concept. The producer and executive won't be seeing the script for at least a few weeks, possibly not for several months. When they see it again, it will no longer be just a concept, but a real, fleshed-out screenplay, and they will have a whole new set of ideas and opinions about it. In the meantime, they have had dozens and dozens of other meetings on other projects and probably hardly remember what they said at the earlier meeting anyway.

Now, obviously, there is some risk involved in playing it this way. If the note they suggested was central to the premise and enormous in scope, and they were adamant about its importance, you are in danger of getting fired as soon as they've seen the first draft. Use your judgment here. Ideas that get tossed around at these meetings are usually off the cuff. They are not usually thought out in great depth. You'll likely be able to tell the difference between casual notes and the ideas to which the higher-ups are passionately married.

If they read the draft and are unhappy about your choices, you can always make changes in the next draft and try it their way. At least you will have had the satisfaction of having written it as well as you possibly could for yourself first.

The Notes Meeting

These are the meetings where input is given after a script has been read. They are probably the longest meetings you will ever sit through. Don't plan anything important immediately following one because, though most last only an hour or two, they can easily stretch to three or four—and will seem like eight or ten.

If the producer and executive have any sensitivity at all, they will begin the meeting with what they liked. The good things. Listen carefully and remember these. I always write down these first positive comments at the top of my pad so I'll remember later while I'm rewriting that it wasn't all bad. I am stressing this because what follows in this meeting are several hours of criticism in minute detail!

As your career progresses and you gain self-confidence as a writer, these meetings will get easier to endure, but at first they can be devastating. I used to think that if the script was good enough, they wouldn't have any notes. They would just say, "Terrific job. We want to shoot in May." But this never happens.

They will always have notes and want to make changes because that is their job. They are paid a lot of money to develop scripts. So you will get lots of notes. And it will often seem by the end of the meeting that if you followed all their notes the script would be decimated.

Ways to Cope

There are many ways to work with and around these notes.

1 Validate their ideas. When they suggest something that you like or that will enhance the script, be sure to tell them you think it's a good idea. (They will fight less for other changes if they feel you are already appreciating and using several ideas of theirs.)

2 Write down all of their notes. Whether you plan to use them or not. Once they see that you have written it down they won't feel like they have to keep repeating it, explaining it, or fighting for it. Writing it down only *implies* that you will do it. Later on, you can see which notes actually will work together.

3 Keep your head. Try to avoid phrases like "Are you out of your *!$%*#$*! mind?!?" Occasionally in an attempt to be off-the-wall brilliant, executives will say outrageous things like, "What if we make the love interest a man and turn it into a buddy movie?" or "What if we moved the whole thing from China to South America?" Comments like these imply that they are virtually throwing out all your hard work and asking for a whole new script. Don't panic. Usually the more outrageous the suggestion, the more risky it is, and therefore the less sure the executive is that you should do it. But if you attack his idea, he will have to defend it or look like a fool. So let it go with a comment like, "I'd have to take some time to rethink things if we were going to change it that radically." But do not suggest that you end the meeting and go home to think it over. Just keep kicking around options other than this wild card.

4 Come up with a new idea yourself. It doesn't matter if it's something you come up with on the spur of the moment or something you've had up your sleeve since you walked in the door. A well-placed "new idea" can effectively change the subject and save everyone from having to get deeply involved in something about which the executive himself is probably already having second thoughts. The phrase "or what if . . . ?" has saved many a screenplay from disaster.

Don't make it too obvious that you are changing the subject just to get away from another topic. When you do this, try to make it seem like something that just came to you. Deliver your suggestion with new enthusiasm.

5 Give them credit. Use a phrase such as "You just gave me a great idea!" When they then ask, "What is it?" they are already hoping to like it so that they can take credit for whatever it is.

6 Don't fight for what they are telling you they don't like. Don't engage in a head-to-head battle over an issue, finding yourself defending something they don't like. This kind of fight just makes them dig more deeply into their trenches. The more staunchly you defend your work, the harder they will try to find reasons why your way is no good. This gets unpleasant fast, and worse, everyone will remember that sore point, so if the script comes back without their recommendations it will be glaringly apparent.

You can say something like, "I guess I didn't pull it off, but what I was trying to do with that scene was . . ." With an opening like this, they may even come in to defend you. Quite possibly they will help you try to come up with a solution for doing it your way.

7 Stay open (try to stay on the same side). Sometimes after a grueling and painful hour or two, an executive will come up with a terrific idea that will solve a lot of your problems. They were hired to do this job for a reason. They are probably more experienced than you—and hey, sometimes miracles do happen. Just be grateful, catch the ball, and run for the end zone.

Remember that the executive's goal is the same as yours: to make the best movie possible. After a couple of hours of taking apart your script, they are going to look a lot like the enemy, so you must work hard to stay open to them, to keep listening. If you don't, they may finally say that one thing that could really help, but you won't even hear it.

8 Your script is going to change. Remember this because it's true. No matter how good your script is, it will be changed. If you want to stay in the game and protect your script as much as possible, your only choice is to make script changes. Not all the changes they suggest, but some of them. If you stubbornly refuse to revise, they will replace you with another writer and you won't even be on the bench. You'll be in the showers either pissed off or crying. It's not always easy, but stay in the game as much as you can.

9 Make up reasons. If one of their off-the-wall ideas is going too far—you can see the match flickering just before the Hindenburg goes up in flames—make up a reason or two why you can't accommodate the suggestion. I know the real reason you don't want to do what they are suggesting is that you would sooner die, but this is not going to go over well.

Try to give technical reasons why the structure will be thrown off, or why their idea is inconsistent with your main character's motivations. Find something that sounds good: a "writer's explanation" why it has to be done the way you are suggesting.

10 Find an ally in the room. There are usually several people in these meetings. At the very least there will be you, your producer, and the studio executive. I've been in meetings where there have been as many as eight, which is a zoo. But if you find your script is being sent up the river into obscurity, try to find someone in the room who might agree with you.

Even though the executive has the power to do whatever he wants, if he comes up against two or (even better) three of you that agree, the chances are he won't overrule all of you. If his suggestions turned out badly, everyone would know it was his fault and (though they probably won't say it) would be in a position to say, "I told you so."

It is perfectly all right to look across at someone else in the room and say, "Jack, what do you think?" But don't do it if there is any chance Jack will be too lily-livered to back you up and instead will side with the exec. Use your intuition and read other people's body language to figure out quickly who might stand behind you. It's not that hard. Often, as you give your impassioned plea, there will be someone nodding in recognition of a good idea.

11 At the end of the meeting. Tell them that you understand their problems, that you think a lot of their suggestions are good, and that you're sure you'll also find other solutions as you rewrite it. This will make it clear that you understood all their notes about what is wrong, but it still gives you some leeway in execution. Or simply say, "This was a good meeting. Good notes. Very helpful. Thank you."

12 If you lose points in the meeting. If you just can't win, be prepared to go home and try to write it their way. Then, if their way doesn't work at all, save the weak pages and rewrite it your way. Bring those discarded pages with you to the next meeting. If they say, "Why didn't you do such-and-such as we discussed?" you can answer honestly, "I tried it and I just couldn't make it work. I brought those pages with me, if you want to read them. I'm sure you'll agree that it just doesn't work."

Then you can either give them the pages or not, as they wish. You will have demonstrated that you have been trying to follow their suggestions, but that the most important thing to you is writing the best possible screenplay.

A Last Thought to Remember

Do not try to do all of everyone's notes. If you try to do every note from every person who was at the meeting, there is a good chance your screenplay is going to end up looking like a patchwork quilt full of clashing fabrics. As you go through the process of rewriting, try to keep an eye on the big picture and use only those notes that contribute to the script as a whole. Use the notes that fit together and support each other. Don't let the notes throw the structure out of balance. Keep your turning points within the classic three-act range. Don't let subplots overpower your main plot line.

You may have to fight to save your screenplay, but I recommend that you fight subversively. Don't let them know you are fighting. You will come out better at the end of these battles if the opposition thinks you are cooperating with them.

PART THREE

Your Screenwriting Career

CHAPTER 15

The Writers Guild of America

The **Writers Guild of America** is the union for writers of movies, television, and radio, with branches in Los Angeles and New York (WGA West and WGA East). Its purpose is to improve working conditions and wages, and to protect the rights of media writers. It also has a strong health care plan at no cost to the writer, and an outstanding pension plan.

Who Is Eligible to Join?

You must have 24 units of credit within a two-year period to join the Guild. Units are given out as follows ("story" means outline, not screenplay).

3 units—Story for 30-minute radio or teleplay

4 units—Story for a theatrical short subject, 30 to 60 minutes.

6 units—Teleplay or radio play, 30 minutes

8 units—Story for radio or teleplay, 60 to 90 minutes

8 units—Short screenplay, 30 to 60 minutes

12 units—Story for radio, TV, or film, 90 minutes or longer

12 units—Script for radio or TV, more than 60 to 90 minutes

24 units—Screenplay for radio, TV, or film, 90 minutes or longer

24 units—Bible for TV series or miniseries, 4 hours long or more

A rewrite gets ½ of the units of credit for each of the above.

A polish gets ¼ of the units of credit.

An option gets ½ of the units of credit.

Writing in collaboration receives full credit for each partner.

The writer must apply for WGA membership by the 31st day of employment. The fee for joining the Guild goes up periodically. In early 2002, it was $2,500. Dues are 1½% of your gross earnings, paid quarterly. If you have no earnings in a particular quarter, your dues for that quarter are $25.

Benefits

Medical/dental insurance. If you earn a minimum of $18,659 per year writing for movies, television, or radio, you are eligible for coverage by the Guild's medical and dental plans. You do not pay for these. Your employers pay the Guild an additional 12½ percent every time they hire you. This money is divided up between the Pension Plan (6%) and the Health Plan (6½%) and costs you nothing. In other words, for every $10,000 the studio (or network) pays you, they pay an additional $1,250 directly to the Guild in your name.

Medical and dental coverage is quite good. It also covers your spouse and children, and includes a discount card for prescription medication. The major medical part of the plan covers "usual, customary, and reasonable charges" for services.

Pension plan. With every job, your employers contribute to your pension plan. If you qualify for the pension plan (earning a required number of earnings points over several years) then at the age of 62, you will receive a monthly check in an amount based on your cumulative WGA earnings, for the rest of your life.

Library. The Guild has a library of scripts which include over 1,000 past winners of the Writers Guild Awards. They also have a viewing facility in the Writer's Guild building and library of DVDs and videos.

Credit union. It is difficult for freelance writers with irregular incomes to establish credit and qualify for loans. The Guild has its own credit union to serve members' needs.

Film society. For a small fee, members can join the WGA Film Society and obtain passes for the writer and a guest to attend screenings at their theater in Beverly Hills of the latest films. This is an excellent value and includes most major movie releases in any given year.

Script registration services. As I mentioned in Chapter 3, for a small fee you can register your script with the WGA ($20 for non-members, $10 for members). They keep registered scripts on file for five years. If someone plagiarizes your work, the registered copy at the Guild can be used as evidence in court.

Minimums. The Guild has established a scale of minimum payments for every kind of writing for movies, television, and radio. This minimum escalates each year in a pre-determined schedule to keep pace with inflation.

Residual collection. The Guild has a watchdog staff whose job it is to monitor all television broadcasts both in this country and worldwide and bill the appropriate companies when your programs or movies are broadcast. These residual checks go directly to the union, which forwards them to you without fees or deductions. This service alone makes up for what most of us pay in dues each year. Residuals are not subject to the 10% agent's fee, so they don't go through your agency at all.

Legal services. If the company you are working for is taking advantage of you and not operating according to Guild regulations (asking for free drafts, delaying payments to you, etc.) you can go the Guild and file a complaint. They have a staff of lawyers who can intercede with these companies on your behalf.

Credit arbitration. Producers and directors are powerless to determine which writer should or should not receive credit on the screen. If they were able to give out screen credits, they could use them as bargaining tools in deal negotiations and rob deserving writers of their due credit.

Which writers' names appear on the screen, in what order, and under what title ("Written By," "Story By," etc.) are decided by arbitration panels of working writers who volunteer their time to anonymously read and evaluate each writer's contribution to the final script.

A panel member receives a copy of each subsequent draft of the script with the writers' names removed, labeled simply Writer A, Writer B, etc. in the order written, ending with the final shooting script. The panel votes on who receives credit.

No more than three writers will finally share the credit. The term "Written By" is only given when the screenplay is original, i.e., not a remake, a sequel, or based on material from another medium.

As mentioned in Chapter 14, the first writer of an original script will almost always receive some kind of screen credit unless his or her contribution has been essentially eliminated in content, story, character, and style.

If the writers agree among themselves who should get credit and in what order, the script does not need to go through the arbitration process, and the agreed-upon writing credits will be the ones to appear on the screen.

Residual and bonus monies are paid based on who gets screen credit. So it is important, even if you hate the film and want your name taken off, that you replace it with a pseudonym. That way, you still receive your money without sacrificing your reputation. For a writer in this town, a credit on almost any film that is produced is better than none.

Occasionally the arbitration process can get extraordinarily complex. There was a rumor that *Tootsie* had 14 writers, all seeking credit. That arbitration panel had to sort out a lot of drafts.

There are safeguards built into the arbitration process to ensure that a producer or director will be unable to take credit for your work.

Strikes

Every three or four years, the Writers Guild contract with "management" (studios, networks, and production companies) expires, and a new agreement has to be negotiated. As of this writing, the last strike was in 1988 and lasted five months. It was so devastating—many of the people involved lost houses, credit ratings, etc.—that both sides have made serious efforts to avert future strikes. In 2001, a strike was predicted but didn't happen. There is no way to predict whether the WGA will go out on strike in the future, but if you are wise you will save and invest as if we were going out on strike every three to five years.

During a strike, you must register all your screenplays in progress that are under contract so there is a record of where you stopped writing when the strike was called. This is, obviously, to ensure against your being accused of working during the strike. The strike only applies to writing for movies, television, and radio. So you are free to write books, plays, articles, and such during a strike if you like.

A strike may last as long as five months or longer. Throughout a strike there are large WGA membership meetings to discuss the issues, with an open microphone on the floor and votes to decide whether to accept management's latest offer.

Writers are expected to march on the picket lines once or twice a week in two-hour shifts. This is actually the fun part, and one of the rare times that writers really get a chance to know each other and swap stories.

A note on scabbing during a writers' strike: The Guild deals severely with anyone trying to break the strike by writing for struck companies. Penalties are stiff. You could seriously endanger your future as a Guild member by scabbing.

Do I Have to Join the Guild?

Yes. It's essential, though not obligatory. Without membership you may find yourself writing only on spec, trying to sell your scripts outright and then losing them to rewriters. Similarly, you might find yourself working only for the lower-budget companies that don't pay union minimums.

If you want to write for good money, to be hired to revise your own screenplay once it is bought, or to work for any of the major studios and television networks, then you need to join the Guild. All major companies and many of the smaller ones are signatory to the Guild. This means that they are contractually barred from hiring writers who are not members of the Guild once those writers have reached the point of eligibility.

I think you'd be foolish not to join the Guild as soon as possible. The pension, medical, and dental benefits alone eliminate half of the drawbacks of being a freelance writer. The dues are modest. Besides, belonging to the Writers Guild of America is synonymous with being a professional screenwriter.

CHAPTER 16

The Green Light: From Script to Film

Finally! Your script is scheduled to be shot. Here's the moment you have been working and waiting for all your life. Now—the fantasy goes—you can lie back on your chaise longue and handle publicity calls begging you to go on Oprah and Jay Leno. Or hang around on location in a canvas chair with your name on the back, watching movies stars magically turn your words into action.

Well . . . not exactly. First, there is more work.

Pre-Production (Colored Pages)

In the preliminary step, the studio puts the script through a "Final Draft" program, and it comes out with all the scenes numbered and the sound and prop cues capitalized. The team begins "breaking the script down" into a shooting schedule, locations, and budget. Now the game of "colored pages" begins. Every set of changes that follows becomes a new set of pages with changes on them, a different color for each set of revisions. There are more than a dozen different colors ranging from Marigold to Buff, always used in the same order. People who work in production know this order by heart. If they last got a set of pink pages and now they're getting green, they know they missed the yellow pages. And on each new set of pages, the latest changes in the current draft are marked with asterisks in the margin. But let's walk through the process, step by step.

1 First the studio hires a director. This person, of course has his/her own opinions about how to "develop" your script. He will put his mark on it, and often for the better. He is thinking entirely of how it will look on film and how they will shoot it. A good director can add a lot of style and visual richness to the script if you listen and use his notes.

Whether they pay you more money to make the director's changes or not depends on a few things. Technically, of course, they are supposed to pay you for every draft. That is your Writers Guild-given right. If there are more steps left in your contract, this will probably be the case. If the changes are cosmetic, or few, or simple, they may ask you to just "take a quick pass" at it for free. This happens all the time. Whether you agree or not is up to you. If you refuse, they may call your agent and negotiate another fee, or they may just make the changes themselves. There is no telling. Some directors are also writers and do the shooting polish themselves. This happens.

Whatever the financial arrangements (or lack thereof), if you want to be in the director's good graces and be welcome on the set (or location) you may want to cooperate with him on these revisions. Usually they are not too drastic.

Occasionally a director will have his own writer who always writes the shooting polishes on all his movies. This is a drag, but unfortunately there's not much you can do about it. More often, the director is grateful to you for having written a script good enough to attract him to the project, and will give you the respect you deserve.

So you make the director's changes—and here's your first color-coded revised pages, say blue, integrated with the original white (unchanged) pages.

2 Next, they hire stars. You will probably have to tailor a role or two to fit the actors playing them. Sometimes a role will be too demanding for a particular actor and the director will discreetly ask you to cut one of the crying scenes. Sometimes you'll get a talented comic actor or actress for a role that was written without much humor. Then if you're smart you'll go back and add a few funny lines or moments, so as not to waste a valuable new asset. The results will usually be good for the script as well as for the actor.

Occasionally you'll get what seem like silly requests. (A female star once assured me that she "never would have married anyone named Willard!" So her husband became a "Richard.")

Working on *Best Friends for Life*, a CBS movie I scripted, Gena Rowlands and Linda Lavin asked me how I would define "best friends." I thought of my own best friend of 20 years and said, "It's like this: You can spend an hour talking to your therapist and cry the whole time. Then you call your best friend and tell her the exact same things and you both end up laughing." They got it and asked me if I could put that into the script, so it became dialogue. And it was a good addition.

These "actor" changes now give us pink pages interspersed throughout the script.

3 Later, there is a "table read" for the principal actors. They sit around a big table with the Director and Writer (you) and Producers and read the whole script straight through so everyone can get a feel for the movie and the players. Out of this read-through, new problems and new possibilities may become clear that hadn't been noticed before. As in live theater, this rehearsal process, as brief as it is, is extremely important for the writing process. And it is greatly preferable to root out problems now rather than discovering a clunky section of dialogue when you're already out on location with the clock ticking and pressure on the actors to "wing it." So you make a lot of notes as they read through your script out loud.

Your ear has heard a thousand times more dialogue than your eye has read. And so it happens that a line of dialogue that looked perfectly fine on the page sounds wrong when it is spoken aloud. (Sometimes a line sounds so much different out loud than it did in my head, I actually have the thought, "who wrote that?")

Before you know it, there it is again—another set of pages—this time we add yellow to the script.

4 Next, they scout locations and things change again. Possibly your winter scenes have to be changed because they are behind schedule, or spring hit early. In either case the snow is gone and there is mud everywhere. Revise. Or they are shooting in Toronto, simulating New York. So Rockefeller Center and the Empire State Building have to be replaced by a flower market or section of Central Park, landmarks easier to duplicate in

Canada. Or done in stock footage (without actors included in those shots) to accommodate the budget.

If you are shooting in August in Vancouver, where it doesn't get dark until 10:30 p.m., most of your night scenes are going to have to be revised to "DAY" or you'll never be able to get your picture shot on schedule. It is hard to make a stalking killer scary in daylight, but it's better to have the writer wrestling with these kinds of problems than the crew. So "stalking killer in daylight" becomes green pages.

5 Once shooting begins, you will get phone calls.

"We've got rain here. Can you give me a couple of lines to cover it?"

"Barry broke his arm. Can you write us a little back story to explain it?"

"I want to do a slow pan of the lab and I need some O.S. dialogue to cover the shot."

"We ran out of time and money and can't shoot scenes 28 to 32. Instead, could she get a letter that wraps it up for us?"

On *Buffalo Girls,* the director, Rod Hardy, called to describe an opening shot that carried Calamity Jane from riding across the plains, arriving at the fort, pan shot of the entire army, Calamity dismounting, walking through one building, out the back, and joining Bartle and Jim with the Sergeant out back. Could I write it for him? Without thinking I blurted out, "You know exactly what you want. Why don't you just shoot it?" He said, "No. I need the pages." Then I realized that, of course, he was right. The studio judges a director partly on how many pages he's shooting per day. Not how many minutes of film. So I wrote it up and fired it off and they shot it just as he described it to me.

And so on, with as many variations on this as things that can and do go wrong (usually more than there are shooting days.) Now, it's lavender pages.

6 And even after the film is in the can. Even then, you occasionally get calls asking for things like a few lines for the background voices in a crowd scene, for example, for the audio looping in post production. Your final script ends up looking like a rainbow that's been fed through a casino shuffling machine.

Production

During the Shoot

As the writer, will you be allowed or invited to be on the set? This depends almost entirely on your relationship with the director and producers. If your film is being shot locally, it is usually fine to go down and hang out on the set or location, if the director agrees to your presence.

One of the key factors is whether or not you were the last writer to work on the script. Unfortunately, if they have hired someone else to do the "shooting polish" or if the director is making those changes, they may feel awkward or embarrassed about having the original writer present. It's no reflection on you, but in those cases it usually doesn't work out for you to be around much.

If your film is being shot on a distant location, as several of mine have been, don't expect them to pay your way. They will pay for the late-night desperate phone calls and the FedEx deliveries, but if you want to go, you will usually be expected to pay your own way.

Buffalo Girls was a four-hour miniseries. It shot for a month in Santa Fe, New Mexico, and then moved to Bath, England, for two more weeks. My expenses were paid to go to New Mexico for the first week of shooting, as they knew they might need changes there. I paid my own way to England, and booked into the same hotel where the cast and crew were staying. During the shoot there, as the producer began to realize how much I was still doing to make their jobs easier by trimming and tailoring the script to locations needs, he felt guilty and picked up my hotel bill. In that case, being happy to be there and glad to help paid off. It was one of the most fun and satisfying working experiences of my life.

The First Day

When you arrive on location, which you will recognize from blocks away by the large number of trucks and trailers, don't expect celebrity parking status. Find a place out of the way that will not be a problem if equipment has to be moved. Then walk in to where the action is going on, usually recognizable in any weather by the intensely bright lights and clusters of burly

Teamsters. Go up to the first person you see and ask him who the First Assistant Director is and to point him/her out to you. Then you walk up to First A.D., who is the person who runs the set and the crew, put out your hand and say, "Hi, John, I'm Cynthia Whitcomb. I wrote the script. How's it going?"

Befriend the First A.D., and you will quickly begin to feel at home on your own movie location. You will find out what scene they are shooting, how it's going, and you may even get a director's chair to sit in. Then you can meet the producer, director, actors. So much time is taken setting up shots that the chances are at any given moment you may not even see the key players anywhere around. The actors are in their trailers, the director may be with them talking through the next scene, the producer is off fighting for a second crane, etc. And you don't want to be standing around like someone who doesn't belong there. You belong there. It's your movie.

Tips to Make Your Presence on Set More Desirable

1 Don't complain to the director about minor changes. If an actor changes a line, or if the way a scene is being shot is not to your liking, don't complain to the director about it unless it is of particular, vital importance to the script that the line or the intention be altered.

Just as second and third drafts of scripts always change, so dialogue always changes some in the mouths of actors. This is often to the detriment of the script, but once in a while they do improve what you've done. My point is, if you make a stink about every word, no one is going to want you around, because they don't have the time and money to keep reshooting a scene because of a single word or phrase. Don't be a stickler. Save your input for the moments that are really critical. If your comment that will actually save the day's shoot comes after your 20 others, they long since have stopped listening to you. Be selective. Choose your battles carefully.

2 Never give notes to an actor behind the director's back. If a performance is going way off the mark, and therefore doing major damage to a character or the story line, talk to the director about it at a moment when he is not pressured with everything else. (There is a lot of down time while the crew sets up the next shot. These are the best times to approach him, not when he is actually shooting a scene.)

Do not go to an actor and suggest a change in performance. Actors may be open to this, but it will damage your relationship with the director. Guiding the performances is his domain. And the strength of your relationship with the director, as I've said, is your backstage pass to the shoot.

3 Keep a low profile. Be absolutely silent during filming. Don't bring a lot of friends along or turn the shoot into your own personal party.

4 Don't get in the way of the technical crew.

5 Don't take snapshots during filming. There will be an opportunity to get a picture of yourself with the stars between set-ups. Not while people are trying to shoot a scene.

6 Don't go running to the producer with criticism of the director. This will backfire on you in no time.

Dailies

This is the term for the uncut footage that was shot the previous day. Dailies are shown each day to executives, producers, the director, and key crew members to be sure that they have the coverage they need and that the scenes they've shot have turned out well. If something needs to be reshot for any reason, they need to know as soon as possible.

Occasionally, if the producer and director agree, the writer is welcome to sit in on dailies. A writer watches these shots from a different perspective than a director or producer. If a key piece of the story gets lost in the shoot, the writer will notice it even when the others may not.

One scene in a movie I scripted was set during a ball at the Russian Embassy, in Paris, circa 1946. There was supposed to have been dialogue spoken during a waltz between two of the main characters. Because it was extremely difficult to shoot the couple as they whirled around the dance floor and have the actors' faces in the shot while they spoke their lines, they just decided to cut them. When I saw the dailies, I pointed out that without those lines, there would be no explanation as to why the young man would seem to disappear from the film, never to be seen again. Everyone immediately recognized the story problem and a pickup shot was scheduled.

If a writer hadn't been there in dailies, this kind of mistake would not have been caught until the rough cut was put together, at which point the picture has wrapped and all the actors have gone home. In other words, impossible to fix. And it would have been one of those story holes that critics later blame on the writer.

Post-Production

Rough Cut to Final Cut

Once shooting is complete, the post-production process begins. As the writer, you will not be part of this process at all, until the premiere or final screenings, unless you ask to be included in the earlier cuts and are invited to attend. Sometimes you can even get to sit in on some of the editing, if you befriend the director or cinematographer.

It can be extremely useful for you to be involved in this process, beginning with the editor's first assemblage, through the rough cut, to the director's cut, and then the final cut which the studio approves. You will notice things, especially in the trimming-down phase, when the film is 20 or 30 minutes too long, that will help ensure that while footage is cut, the story line and character development will suffer only minimal damage.

The director and editor spend all day every day, and many nights as well, watching this footage over and over again. They can't help but lose some of their perspective and assume that an audience knows certain things just because they know them so well, even though the necessary exposition may have disappeared on the cutting-room floor.

In addition to helping maintain the integrity of the story by watching all the early versions, you will also learn a great deal about the filmmaking process that can be learned in no other way. How a story is told in images, how cutting from one image to the next implies things to an audience, and how if an actor conveys certain feelings in a look, it is best to cut lines meant to convey the same information but which now are superfluous.

"Show, don't tell" is the golden rule of film making. This experience will be invaluable later if and when you move into producing and directing.

Screenings

Almost every new feature film and television movie has at least one private screening for friends and/or press before it opens commercially. A production assistant will ask you for the names of people you want to include on the invitation list. These screenings are often held at the Academy, Director's Guild Theater, or on one of the studio lots.

The reaction at the screening is generally the best you'll ever have. Almost everyone in the audience either worked on the picture or is friends with someone who did.

There is an old saying that a movie is never as good as its dailies or as bad as its rough cut. This is because the dailies include all the possibilities; you are seeing it all. And the rough cut is usually a mess, with lighting mismatched, sound effects and music missing, and the timing off. Try not to judge your film until you see it with all the rough edges smoothed out, the color matched, the music and sound cues in place. And let's not forget the most thrilling part: the titles. Your name on the big screen.

The writer's name will always come at the beginning of a film unless there are no opening credits. If the director's name is at the end, then so is the writer's, but usually both come at the beginning. In terms of prestige, the later in the opening credits, the better. (Not for actors, of course, which is the reverse.) The last title card will be the director's. Immediately preceding his will probably be the producer's. The writer's credit is usually third from last.

I learned early on that when people come up to you and congratulate you or compliment you at the end of these screenings, it is pointless to do anything but thank them and say no more. Even if what is on the screen is nothing like you intended and you want to scream, "That is not my movie!" Saying anything more than a polite "thank you" makes you look and feel like an idiot.

Later on, in the solitude of your home, you can confide to those nearest and dearest what your true feelings are. But not in public.

Reviews

John Gardner writes in *On Moral Fiction*, "The trouble with our present criticism is that criticism is, for the most part, not important. It treats the only true magic in the world as if it were done with wires."

You must not take reviews too seriously. If you read enough of them, you'll find that they are always mixed. There has almost never been a movie made that didn't get both good and bad reviews. I know it can be painful, especially if one of the bad reviews is printed in your hometown paper, where your family and all your old high-school buddies live, but reviews don't mean very much.

My first TV movie, *Leave 'Em Laughing*, got almost entirely good reviews and was nominated for several prestigious awards, including the Humanitas. *Variety* said, "a fine, warming experience thanks to a perceptive teleplay by Cynthia Whitcomb . . . It's a stirring event." About the same movie, however, the *Washington Post* said: "Cynthia Whitcomb is not ready for the big time. In fact she may not be ready for the small time." I threw the *Post* away immediately. All right, so it sort of stuck in my memory. I have since learned to forget them more thoroughly. We live and learn.

My point is, you can't take the reviews seriously. Every reviewer's taste is different. Paste the good ones in your scrapbook and bury the bad ones under the dog-food cans and dirty diapers.

The Numbers

In the New York Theater, you know you've got a hit by reading the *New York Times*. Not so in Hollywood. Most of us read the reviews, but they in no way affect the way we measure success.

The Industry measures success strictly by the numbers. How much did a picture gross its opening weekend? What were the overnight ratings of a TV show? What were the national Nielsons? This is how you know if you're a hit in this town.

If in the first weekend of wide release (across the country) a movie does $25 million or more, it's a hit. (Unless it cost more than $40 million and dies the second weekend.) For a lower-budget picture, half that amount in an opening weekend could still mean a hit. $100 million dollars is still the magic number, the club everyone wants to get into. (Desperately, if your picture cost nearly that much to make.)

In television, you shoot for the Top Ten for the week, and hopefully a 20 share or better. These numbers have shrunk significantly over the last ten years or so as television has been divided into many times more channels that split the audience. In TV you want to "take the night," i.e., beat out the other two networks' prime-time programming for that night.

As recently as 1989 when I co-wrote a miniseries for NBC, *I Know My First Name Is Steven,* you could pull in phenomenal numbers for certain kinds of television events. That two-nighter did a 35 share the first night and a 42 the second. In other words, 42% of all television sets in America were watching our show that second night. We'll never see those kind of numbers again. A dozen years later, we are already looking back on those days as a golden era of television programming.

If your movie gets made, whether it's a hit or a disaster, it is going to be good for you as a writer. Your price will go up. Your prestige, as well. For a director, it can be very bad for future employment to have made a turkey. For a writer, though, the main thing, in terms of getting work, is that your movies get made.

A finished film is a completely different animal from a finished screenplay. It will always fail to live up to the movie that was in your mind during the process of creation. Julius Epstein was disappointed in the way *Casablanca* turned out.

Sometimes they will break your heart. Sometimes they will be so much better than you feared they might be that you will be thrilled. And sometimes you may be just simply thrilled. Every now and then, things do go right.

One of the questions people often ask is, "Why are there so many bad movies?" In fact, there are so many things that can go wrong that directly affect the final product that the real miracle is that there are so many good ones. You know my point of view about this by now. You do the best work you can. Then you win some and you lose some. But you win *some.*

CHAPTER 17

Hyphenation: Producing and Directing Your Own Scripts

Why do more than write? After working so hard and long to establish a career as a screenwriter, now that you have arrived and are making good money, why not be satisfied and stop there?

Well, because there are just so many movies you can bear to watch them shoot, powerless to help really shape and cast them, before you have to try to assert more control over the creative process. It is your vision. It's only natural to want to make it come out as close as possible to the original movie in your mind.

Associate Producing

"Associate producer" is a catchall title, often used as merely a kicker in a deal to make a writer feel more important. This title may or may not even come with any additional money. It can be strictly a nominal arrangement like an honorary doctorate. "Your name is on the screen twice; now be satisfied and stay out of the way."

If your goal is to produce, it must be clarified from the negotiation of the deal just what your job will be as associate producer. Let your agent ask the questions and give you the answers. Will you be in on casting sessions? Will you be consulted in the choice of director? Locations? Art director? Cinematographer? Will your expenses be paid to go on location?

If your attitude as associate producer is to learn all you can, then befriend the UPM (Unit Production Manager). He knows everything and really runs most of the show. If he likes you, he can be a gold mine of information.

Producing (Line Producing)

What they call the "line producer" is the producer on the front line, actually making the movie. He is responsible for everything. It's the producer's job to make sure that the script gets written and the picture gets made, that everyone does his job, that the movie is on schedule, on budget, that everyone gets fed and takes union-dictated breaks, that locations are ready, sets are dressed, that actors show up, that helicopters are rented, and cranes and special effects and stuntmen and extras—and *all of it*. Get the idea?

I first really understood what the producer's job was when I was on location shooting one of my earliest movies (obviously I can't tell you which one) and the star pitched a fit and refused to come out of his trailer. I was alarmed and asked the director what he was going to do. He smiled tensely, sat down in his director's chair, pulled out his cell phone, and dialed the producer. And these are the exact words he said: "You've got a problem."

All problems are basically the producer's problems to solve. All they do, before, during, and after production is put out fires. All day, every day, and most nights. It is not a job for wimps. The producer is the problem solver, the boss, the bank, and the last word. He is the link between the studio and the team. If this were a war, he'd be the liaison in the field between the Pentagon and the beaches of Normandy.

It is not difficult for a bright, assertive, successful writer to cross over into being a producer, but there are a few drawbacks. A friend of mine who is a successful producer told me that the hardest part of producing is being willing to be the person that nobody likes. During the 1988 WGA strike, David Letterman coached his live audience to respond in unison to the query "And what are the producers?" Audience: *"Money-sucking slime!"*

Producers work horrendous hours under extraordinary pressure, get ulcers, high blood pressure, divorced, and almost no sleep that isn't plagued with nightmares of helicopter crashes or *Battlefield Earth*.

Executive Producing

The executive producer is usually the initiator. He sets up the whole movie. He finds the project, buys a book, a play, rights to a true story, or an original screenplay and takes it from square one. He brings the elements together, from development through pre-production all the way through post-production, publicity, and distribution. From setting it up with a studio to developing the script and attaching a director, line producer, and stars.

And he guarantees the back end. In other words, he is the one who ultimately is responsible if the film goes over budget. We generally think of executive producers as the money people. They are the ones who come up with the funds one way or another. The exec producer may drop by the set once a week to see how things are going and perhaps boost morale. He or she may not be deeply involved in the day-to-day details of the filmmaking process. Or they may be there every minute.

All producing titles and duties vary quite a bit from deal to deal and producer to producer. If the film wins the Best Picture Oscar, the executive producer is the guy who gets to keep the little gold man.

Directing

After stardom, the most glamorous, sought-after job in filmmaking is directing. Directors have enormous prestige if their films are good, or successful, or both. So how do writers become directors?

Many writers have become directors. The kind of vision that creates the images on the page is not so different from the vision that translates them onto film. James L. Brooks, Oliver Stone, Lawrence Kasdan, Woody Allen, Philip Kaufman, Barry Levinson, Curtis Hanson, Cameron Crowe, the Cohen brothers—all were screenwriters first and still are screenwriters. Let's not forget that George Lucas wrote *Star Wars*.

How did these writers get the chance to direct? It's not complicated. Here's one way:

- Write a picture that gets shot and is at least moderately successful.
- Write another screenplay on the heels of that success that several major studios are chomping at the bit to get hold of.
- Make the sale of that hot screenplay contingent on them letting you direct it.

There are other ways to break into directing that don't involve writing at all. Making a low-budget film that wins prizes at film festivals. Shooting music videos. Shooting commercials. But for a writer, the most practical, direct, and least expensive road to directing movies is to come straight out of film school with an impressive student film under one arm and a hot, marketable feature-film screenplay under the other.

TV Hyphenates

Crossing over into other jobs beyond writing is actually easier in television than in feature films. This is primarily because budgets are lower, so the financial risk of hiring a new director or producer is not as great. An average TV movie budget is around $5 million, while feature films these days often cost ten times that much.

If you are a TV series staff writer, it is not unreasonable to hope for an opportunity to direct an episode, especially in the second or third season. And occasionally TV movie directors get opportunities to direct feature films.

Once you have several screen credits to your name, there are possibilities to expand your career and try on a few other hats.

CHAPTER 18

Staying Sane and Happy in a Crazy Business

You are on the way. Here are a few parting ideas I want to leave with you. First, don't take it too seriously. Remember, it's only a movie. Nothing that ever happened or didn't happen in Hollywood is worth killing yourself over. Believe me. People take it pretty seriously, but it isn't a serious business when it comes right down to it. It's magic and make-believe. Colored light filtered through a moving strip of plastic.

And it truly is a crapshoot. But guess what? You get to roll the magic dice as hard, fast, and often as you have the heart for. One shot at the Big Casino is a lie. Take as many shots as you want. Casinos never close. Shake 'em, blow on 'em, and let 'em fly.

Pressures seem to abound out here in Movieland. One thing to keep in mind as you are tearing your hair out trying to make a script deadline: Given the choice, they'd rather have it good than fast. It will not ruin your reputation if you call and say "I need a few more days." Or what I usually say: "It's going great and I need a few more days." (I am a fiction writer, after all, and this makes us all feel better.) Writing is not bricklaying, and the people you will be working for understand that. Later, they never remember if it was late. They only remember if it was good.

It's also time to start treating yourself like a professional screenwriter. Let's face it, a lot of us became writers because we wanted to be writers as much as because we wanted to write. We wanted to be Ernest Hemingway and Lillian Hellman and Dashiell Hammett and Dorothy Parker.

If you think that a real writer writes on yellow legal pads with a fountain pen in Italian restaurants at two in the morning, go out and buy the pen and find the restaurant. See how it feels. If you think that real writers wear Irish fisherman sweaters and English leather walking shoes, buy the shoes.

Invest in yourself. Feel the part. I have done all the things that I thought writers should do, from living in France to living in poverty, from the fountain pens to the sidewalk cafés. This is not merely pretense, but a way of living out the stirrings of our imaginations. And if you're a writer, you already know about the magical powers of your own imagination.

You need to believe that you are a writer and feel proud to be one.

There are dozens of other things you can do. Take workshops and seminars. If the WGA goes on strike, go down and march on the picket lines. Nobody cares that you are not a member. They will love the support. Grab a picket sign, get to know the other members, and be one of them. You might even find a mentor to take you under his or her wing. Read books and screenplays and go to the movies with your notebook and stopwatch. Do it all.

Do the best work you possibly can and then, no matter what else happens to it, you will have the satisfaction that comes from doing good solid work.

Above all, as you make your way through the nonsensical, meandering path of a Hollywood screenwriting career, no matter what you encounter, don't let it kill off your love of movies. Especially those most private screenings that play first and best on the movie screen of your mind.

Preserve and defend your own magic. It is finally the only thing of real value you have to offer.

Remember:

Work hard.

Take chances.

Be very, very bold.

PART FOUR

Epilogue

CHAPTER 19

A True Screenwriting Cinderella Story

I know that one reason you bought a book on selling screenplays is that you're looking for that true story of the one writer that hit the longshot and won the spec-script Hollywood lottery. So here is your story. It's a true story about a regular guy who got that big break, sold his screenplay for a million dollars and had two movies filmed in that first year: *Finding Forrester* (starring Sean Connery) and *The Rookie* (starring Dennis Quaid). And two more pictures will begin shooting before the second year is out.

I will let Mike Rich tell his remarkable story in his own words. Here is a bedtime story for you to dream on as you tuck yourself in at night.

Once upon a time, there was this Portland, Oregon, morning drive-time D.J. . . .

Mike Rich

I've always had an interest in writing, dating back to high school.

The stories of most good writers begin with a great teacher, and for me it was Sharon Forster in high school. She was a wonderful English teacher who drove me and inspired me to write. In those days it was primarily short stories.

I kept that interest into adulthood. I went into radio broadcasting. But I was a young parent and didn't have time for anything longer than short stories. It wasn't until around 1994 or so when I first got interested in trying a screenplay, and that was primarily driven by my love for film.

I was like most people who think, "I've got a great idea for a screenplay." So I looked at the books and did everything wrong. I had the margins and the format all wrong.

But one thing I did that really helped me was that I read screenplays. They were just becoming available then. I found movies that I really enjoyed, movies that had inspired me and touched me, and then I found the screenplays and read them.

And then I wrote. I found out very quickly that there's much more to writing a screenplay than just having a good idea. The first screenplay I wrote, I got 60 pages into it and then realized that there weren't 60 more pages. That was it.

It went into a drawer.

I tried again. The second one, I got through the whole script and finished it. And it was truly awful. But I still have that screenplay, bound right next to the other ones for *Finding Forrester* and *The Rookie*, because it really served a purpose. I think you have to give yourself permission to write a bad screenplay before you can write a good one.

I truly enjoyed it. For me it was a hobby. I viewed it as a hobby. At that time I wasn't approaching it as a potential career. It was a creative outlet the way playing a guitar would be for someone else. Because of the hours I was putting in at KINK-FM, there were only a couple of hours a day when I could write. And I took advantage of those hours. I was very disciplined.

I was a Monday-through-Friday guy at KINK-FM radio in Portland, Oregon. It's half music and half NPR and news. I was the news half of a broadcasting team with Les Sarnoff. I anchored the news Monday through Friday.

I'd get up at about 2:30 a.m. to get to the radio station by 3:15. The morning show would start at 5:00 and go till 9:00. I'd be at the station until around 11, then would go home, have lunch, and catch a short nap.

And then I'd write until the kids got home from school. I'd get two hours of writing in, sometimes three. I wrote on weekends as well. Those were the golden days. I'd get up early so I wouldn't be taking weekend afternoons away from my family.

The story for the third screenplay was actually inspired by an interview I did on the air with an author. We were talking about how authors in the first half of the century were like rock stars. They were an eccentric and reclusive bunch. This author was telling me how they put up a barrier around themselves, and no one got through that barrier. And after that interview I found myself thinking about what would happen if someone got through that barrier.

And that was the germ of the idea for *Finding Forrester.*

I didn't begin writing for several weeks after that. I let it work itself around in my head, which is kind of my unorthodox way of writing. I gradually get to a point where I benchmark everything out. I surprisingly didn't do very much outlining; but I spent enough time and had such a feel for the story that I didn't do much of that. It's not something I recommend, but I didn't have to do much of it on that one.

It took about four months. Finished it. Felt that there was a good story there and was very much aware that the screenplay was better than the screenplays I'd written before. But I knew that it wasn't where it needed to be, so I spent another eight months rewriting it—with no direction on what it needed to be. Rewriting from the gut. The screenplay got in better shape and then I sent it out.

I had never even thought about sending my first screenplays out, but this one I was more confident about.

I sent it out to probably a couple dozen production companies, all the major agencies and studios, and didn't get one person to read it. It just came back.

Sometimes it would come back *unopened.*

But I don't think I was discouraged because I was very much aware of the long odds of a screenplay selling.

But I did ask a friend of mine, David Wilson, who was with the Oregon Film Board at the time, if he had any suggestions. And his advice was very straightforward. He said, "Mike, if you feel strongly about the project, try entering it in a competition."

So I did. This was in 1998, and it was pretty close to the deadline. It was April when I got this advice and the first deadline was in May. So I entered it in the Nicholl Fellowship, and in the Austin Film Festival Competition.

What's kind of ironic about the story is that the first letter I got was from Austin. And I didn't make the cut.

And I remember getting the first letter from the Nicholl Fellowship, completely anticipating it being a similar letter to the one I'd already gotten from Austin—and it wasn't. It said I'd been selected as a quarter-finalist.

To this day that was one of the best days for me because it represented independent validation that this was pretty decent.

I remember going on the air that first day and saying to my partner, "Les, I have to tell you about this letter I got. I entered this screenwriting contest and I'm a quarter-finalist." I thought that would be the last we'd hear about it.

Then began a few months of anticipation and waiting, and then elation, as letters kept coming. I went on to tell Les on the air about being a finalist, and then making the final cut and winning the Nicholls Fellowship in October 1998.

And all the listeners became live participants in my story. They followed it from the very beginning all the way through.

That year, there were 4,500 screenplays entered in the Nicholls, which was a high. This year, 2002, they had more than 6,000 scripts. It is set up to help writers that have never sold a screenplay and can't get anyone to read it. The entry fee then was $35.

And there were five winners. They give a $25,000 fellowship and their goal is to encourage people to continue writing, to take time off from their profession to write another screenplay. So they give you a check for $5,000 at the banquet, and then they continue to send you $5,000 quarterly.

When I got the phone call saying that I was a fellowship winner, it was still about four or five weeks before the banquet was held. The five names of the Fellowship winners were printed in *Variety*.

And the floodgates opened. There were no messages on my phone one day—then *Variety* came out. And that day, there were 80 messages on my machine. And they were from all the people that I had been trying to contact. All the people who had sent *Forrester* back unread.

And among those messages were calls from all four of the major agencies, CAA, UTA, William Morris, and ICM.

It was such a wonderful thing. Even though all the production companies were asking me to submit the script to them directly, I quickly decided to get an agent first.

So I took a trip to L.A. And it was interesting. The 10% agent's fee is mandated by California state law, so you don't have to negotiate that. All I had to do was find the agency that had a similar passion for representing my work like the passion I had for writing it.

A couple of the agencies were really interested in *Finding Forrester*, but I was now starting to look beyond that first script. United Talent was the one agency that had that same view. Billy Rose, at UTA, was the guy I chose—although he's not in the business any more. But at the time, he was very passionate not only about representing *Forrester*, but about representing *me*.

For me that made it.

You have to understand that I didn't go down there and buy an Armani suit or anything like that. I just went down in my jeans and my Nike shirt and I said: this is me. I never tried to be anything that I wasn't.

I took a shuttle from the airport. I knew where Wilshire Boulevard was and where Santa Monica was and I knew how to get stuck on the 405. And that was about it.

I flew home and made my decision. I called Billy Rose at UTA and told him I wanted him to represent me. And then things started happening very fast. Within a week the screenplay had sold. This was before the banquet for the Nicholl Fellowship even took place.

UTA called me up and said they were sending the script out to a select group of producers and studios. They kept it very small to try to generate heat on the script. I asked them how long the process would take and they said, "It moves much faster than you think."

The next morning I got a phone call saying they had received their first bid. I said "What does that mean?" They said, "Well, it means—number one—

that your screenplay will sell. Now we just have to determine who it will sell to and for how much."

I asked, "How long will that take? Will we be done by the end of the week?"

They said, "We'll be done by the end of the day. Go about your business. Take your nap."

But there was no sleep that afternoon.

I was actually in my car, stuck on traffic on the 217, when I got the call that they had an offer from Columbia Pictures, ironically one of the studios that had sent me a rejection letter early on. The offer was for $900,000.

It was actually a two-picture deal for *Finding Forrester* and a blind second script for a picture to be named later. The $900,000 was just for *Forrester*—$450,000 against $900,000. Meaning if they shot it, I'd get $900,000. But what happened along the way was that they hired me for so many rewrites that I got extra steps, and by the time it was all done I made around $1,200,000 just for *Forrester*.

The second one, the blind deal, was key because it establishes your quote, or your price as a gun for hire. A spec script sale does not establish that rate. The second one was for $250,000 against $600,000, which did set my price.

That second deal never got exercised. It just went away. By the time the year was up, I had gone on to other things and that $250,000 price became obsolete. *The Rookie* came along, which nearly doubled that quote. Then another project came along with Revolutions Studios that raised that quote even more. That picture didn't get made, but *The Rookie* did. And all of this happened in the course of that year.

The blind deal worked like this. The studio brings you ideas and you bring them ideas. And if you can't agree on one, then the deal expires and you don't do that blind deal. That's the way mine worked. Sometimes they are "pay or play" and you get paid even if you don't find a project, but mine wasn't one of those. And it turned out not to matter.

Getting back to the Nicholl Fellowship, as it turned out the banquet took place after the auction and *Forrester* had sold. It was held at the Beverly Wilshire Hotel right there on Wilshire Boulevard, the *Pretty Woman* hotel. At that point, when I flew down for the banquet, I knew what was in store financially for me with *Forrester*. And I found out when I got down there, that once you have become a professional screenwriter, which I had suddenly become, you don't get the Fellowship money.

It was funny. They looked at me—and after I told them about everything that had happened in those weeks, I said, "Well, I think it's worked out okay." And of course if it weren't for them, none of that would have happened.

To this day I am so grateful to the Foundation for that program, because it has been the stepping-off place, not just for me, but for so many of us. Suzannah Grant who wrote *Erin Brockovich*. Andrew Marlow. A talented young writer/director named Karen Montcrief who had a hit at Sundance this year with *Blue Car*. She was one of the five in my group.

The keynote speaker that night was Curtis Hanson, who is so cool. One of the things I love about Curtis Hanson is that he has a real respect for old Hollywood. A lot of the younger winners at the banquet may not even have been aware of some of the great old Hollywood legendary writers who were there. Daniel Tarradash, who wrote *From Here to Eternity*. John Gay, *Sometimes a Great Notion*. Legendary writers. It was a thrill.

I was 39 when I won and I was the elder statesman of the fellowship winners. Jacob Estes was actually still a senior in college at USC film school. A couple of others were in their thirties.

A few weeks after *Forrester* sold, shortly after the banquet in November, the studio called me up and told me that Sean Connery had expressed interest in the role of William Forrester.

I had never thought about him, because I had imagined Forrester as an American author, someone like Robert Duvall. But as soon as Sean Connery came onboard, not only as the lead, but as executive producer, he became *Forrester* for me. And then I couldn't imagine anyone else.

I had a great relationship with him. One of the things he'd do at rehearsal read-throughs was if there was a dialogue passage he didn't love, he'd write G.S.B. in the margin, which stood for "Get Something Better." He never suggested what the "something" was. But in the part where Forrester edits the boy's writing in his notebook, Sean Connery did suggest the use of the word "constipated" scrawled in the margin. Which was perfect. I never would have thought of that word in a million years.

Breaking into this industry, they don't teach you anything. You either know it or you don't. There is no Hollywood 101. Fortunately Gus Van Sant, the director of *Finding Forrester*, was the kind of guy I could approach with questions. If he'd say something like "We're going to shoot this on a practical location"—I didn't know what a "practical location" was, so I'd ask him. It means it's a real building. I think I endeared myself to some people on the shoot because I was like a 12-year-old kid walking around.

We filmed half of *Forrester* in Toronto. And the first day of rehearsal, I walked on the set they had built of William Forrester's apartment. And it was the oddest feeling. Almost like a magic trick. Because the words I had written describing his apartment had been realized. Literally. Joe DiMaggio's autographed baseball was right where I said it was. And the painting slightly askew on the wall—there it was, slightly askew. The roll-top desk. Everything. It makes you see the power of your words. For the production people it becomes gospel. If you say something's in the room, they put it in the *room*.

While Forrester was my first film, it was Sean Connery's 70th. This is a man who is keenly aware of what will work. He would come to me and say, "This line won't get a laugh." I'd say, "I think it will." Or he'd tell me when something *would* get a laugh. And every one he said would get a laugh, did get a laugh. And the ones I fought for and said would get a laugh, did not get a laugh. He was right. He knows when they're going to laugh.

The Nicholls Fellowship banquet was in November of 1998 and I stayed with the radio job at KINK until June of 2000. And you have to understand that we started production on *Forrester* in *April* of 2000.

I was reluctant to throw everything in. I just didn't know if I'd ever sell another screenplay. There have been a lot of one-hit wonders, and I didn't know if I'd be able to sustain a career.

But by the time we were shooting *Forrester*, and *The Rookie* was in the wings, I was having to go to the radio-station management too often and ask for time off for the movie-career stuff. The radio station was so supportive. I think they enjoyed the ride almost as much as I did. But it got to a point where I wasn't being fair to myself or the radio station, so I finally left.

The great thing about being on the set of *The Rookie* was that the director, John Lee Hancock, was a writer. He had written *Midnight in the Garden of Good and Evil* and *A Perfect World*. And this was his feature film directorial debut.

I had learned some things on the set of *Forrester*, but for that, we were a little bit under the gun going for a holiday release date. It was a tight, tight schedule. With *The Rookie* it was a little more relaxed and we had plenty time. It was great to watch someone learn to direct a movie. With *The Rookie*, I had described these wide open vistas of West Texas and then, there you are.

Moving to L.A. never really came up. Because *Finding Forrester* happened so fast and then *The Rookie* came right after it. And they both got green lights. So there was no need to move to L.A.

The only time it's come up is when I was approached to work in television. To take the step a few other film writers have taken over the last few years—like Aaron Sorkin and Alan Ball—and write a pilot for a TV series. But to be a show runner, you really have to live in L.A., so I wasn't really tempted to do that.

Writing features and living in Oregon hasn't been a problem. They fly me down first-class. They spend money. I have flown to L.A. for a 20-minute meeting that could easily have been done on the phone. They have a car pick you up at your house, they fly you down first-class, and then a car picks you up and drives you to the meeting.

I was lucky enough to cross that line very quickly, where you don't have to be in L.A. seeking out projects because the projects are seeking you. So I haven't thought about moving. I've got three kids and my family loves living in Oregon.

My major indulgence was that I got a really cool red sports car and a great set of golf clubs. I kind of flinched, thinking, you know—a 40-year-old guy buying a red sports car. But my wife encouraged me. She said, "If you're going to get a sports car, get a *sports* car." So I did and it's great. A Lexus SC430 convertible.

So far I've never been replaced on a screenplay. I've been lucky on that. *Radio,* which was my fourth development deal, started out as a Warner Brothers project. When I finished the first draft, they decided that they didn't want to develop it for a number of reasons. So it went into turnaround and was picked up by Revolution Studios, whom I had worked with before on my third project, which hasn't been made.

Radio is the nickname of one of the characters and isn't actually about the radio business at all. A lot of people said, "Hey, so you finally wrote a movie about the radio business." But it's not. It's based on a true story about a Southern championship football coach who befriends a mentally challenged black man. It's a great story. It's set to film in the fall starring Ed Harris and Cuba Gooding.

The next one is set to shoot about a month later. It's called *Miracle* and is the story of the 1980 Olympic hockey team. It was such a pleasure to write because it was really a defining moment for the baby boomers. It was so much more than just a hockey game. It came at a time when the cold war was at its worst, gas supplies were low, there were hostages in Iran, the Soviets had invaded Afghanistan. It was kind of a low point for American self-esteem.

And then you have this ragtag bunch of young American amateur college kids taking on the big bear of the Soviet Union in a hockey game. It was a defining moment for that generation. It certainly was for me. And to get to write that story was a thrill.

It's not cast yet. It will be a young cast. It's tough with hockey—you have to choose between actors who play hockey or hockey players who can act. We're working on that. And we haven't cast the lead role of Herb Brooks, the coach, yet.

Now I don't write on the weekends any more, unless I'm absolutely up against a deadline. Because you can't do it seven days a week. You know how a physical fitness trainer will push you hard for four days and then tell you to rest for a couple of days? It's like that.

People talk about the glamour of screenwriting—and don't get me wrong, it *is* glamorous. At a New York premiere of a movie, when they call your name and you stand up and get acknowledged as the writer by people that you respect, it is glamorous. Or sneaking into a movie theater to watch an audience respond to something you wrote. But it is also hard, hard work. Walking into your office with a blank screen looking at you.

If you have confidence in your story and confidence in your approach, you'll be okay.

One of the real high points brings me back to my high school English teacher, Mrs. Forster. I didn't call her up right away. She lives in Enterprise, Oregon, and I thought it might be a little presumptuous for me to call and say "Hey, I'm writing this screenplay that no one's ever going to see, but I used your name for the main character as a tribute for all you did for me."

But as soon as the script sold I called her. And it was a wonderful phone call. She taught for 27 years in the Enterprise School District. And if there was a Mr. Holland at Enterprise High, it was her. She'd take students on field trips to the Ashland Shakespeare Festival and all those things.

Hers was a typical story. The funding got low and she couldn't do all those things any more. She retired young, and I think when you do that you always wonder if what you did made a difference.

So it was great to call her and tell her about the movie. And it meant a lot to her.

We had a local Portland premiere, with searchlights, out at Lloyd Center, and I invited Mrs. Forster. And at the end of the screening, I introduced her and she stood up. And I think everybody thought, "Oh, she's so young." Everybody applauded and that was pretty great.

What can I say? So far, it's been a great ride. I feel very blessed.

PART FIVE

Appendices

Twenty Things You Can Do to Advance Your Career

To wrap things up, let's recap in the form of a "To Do" list you can use to get into action whenever you need a little kick in the pants to get you moving.

1 See it. Make it real for yourself. Visualize casting, billboard, ad line, etc. Unless it's real for you, you can't sell it to someone else.

2 Learn it. Take screenwriting classes. Read screenwriting books and magazines. Read a screenplay a week. Study a favorite screenwriter or director by renting all of their movies one week and creating a personalized seminar for yourself. You can learn what they know by studying them.

3 Join/form a screenwriting support/critique group. Get the support you need to keep you writing, rewriting, and polishing until your script shines.

4 Register your script with the WGA. And tack the registration slip over your computer. Subscribe to the WGA magazine, *In Print*, and start tuning in to the group you are striving to become a part of.

5 Write a dynamite cover letter. Don't apologize for anything. Tell them why they're going to love it. Include the details about yourself that make it clear you are the only person in the world who can best tell this great story.

6 Make a list of 12 people to send it to. Agents, producers, directors, even actors. Do your homework and make a list that inspires you! Read video packages; read movie credits. Once you find the names, call the Writers Guild, Producer Guild, or Screen Actors Guild and get contact information.

7 **Send it to those 12 people.** Make a chart of who and when. Follow up by phone or e-mail in 3 to 4 weeks.

8 **Enter screenwriting contests.** All the big ones. And any of the smaller ones that appeal to you. Research contests on the Internet and through the ads and announcements found in screenwriting magazines.

9 **See a movie with other screenwriters.** Afterwards, deconstruct and "fix it." What worked? What almost worked? How could it have been better? Talk through new moments or endings that you create.

10 **Read the credits on movies you love.** Make notes. If you loved this Richard Curtis or Tom Stoppard script, what else has he written? Rent them.

11 **Track movie markets.** (*Entertainment Weekly*, etc.) Notice how long certain movies stay in the theaters. Which are disappearing from your local Cineplex? Which have "legs" in the current marketplace?

12 **Start your next script as soon as this one is sent out.** I mean it—the next day! This means you. Even if it's just making a few notes and going to the library to pull a few books on swordfighting.

13 **Practice pitching your stories.** In the mirror. To your dog. To your mom. To anyone. You're a storyteller. Tell those stories.

14 **Think about long-term career goals and write them down.** Have a vision for your career: one year from now. Five years. Ten years.

15 **Ask agents'/producers' assistants for their names.** And write them down!

16 Spend 15 minutes a day on your career. Forcing yourself to come up with things to do in those 15 minutes will break your mind out of the box. You will get creative. You will find new ways to find a crack in the wall. Part of that wall is in your head. You think it's hard to break into Hollywood. This 15 minutes will start to break that up. Then you can conduct a full frontal attack on the wall out there in Hollywood.

17 Don't set a time limit. Plan your career as if it were your life.

18 Get an outfit. Get an outfit you can pitch in or wear to meetings that is professional and comfortable, that makes you feel successful, not self-conscious.

19 Plan a selling trip to L.A. If you were going to L.A., what flights are there? How much do they cost? Where would you stay? Where to rent a car? Print out maps (free on the Internet) from LAX to Paramount, Warner Brothers, Universal. Imagine driving through those gates and telling the guard your name.

20 Rent movies you have loved and watch them again. Watch movies in the style you are going for in your own script. Track down the screenplays and study them. Re-inspire yourself about why you want to do this.

Keep your spirits up. Don't take it too seriously. Rejections are not nearly as important as wins and are unavoidable. The competition is narrowing. The road leads only to success. Keep moving forward one step at a time.

APPENDIX B

Resources: Organizations

Academy of Motion Picture Arts and Sciences
    8949 Wilshire Blvd.
    Beverly Hills, CA 90211
    (310) 247-3000
    www.oscar.com

Academy of Television Arts and Sciences
    5220 Lankershim Blvd.
    North Hollywood, CA 91601
    (818) 754-2800
    www.emmys.tv

American Film Institute
    2021 North Western Ave.
    Hollywood, CA 90027
    (323) 856-7600
    www.afionline.org

Directors Guild of America
    7920 Sunset Blvd.
    Los Angeles, CA 90046
    (310) 289-2000
    www.dga.org

Producers Guild of America
    6363 Sunset Blvd., 9th floor
    Los Angeles, CA 90028
    (323) 960-2590
    www.producersguild.org

Screen Actors Guild
    5757 Wilshire Blvd.
    Los Angeles, CA 90036-3600
    (323) 954-1600
    www.sag.org

Women in Film
  8857 West Olympic Blvd., Suite 203
  Beverly Hills, CA 90211
  (310) 657-5144
  www.wif.org

Writers Guild of America
  7000 W. Third
  Los Angeles, CA 90048
  (323) 951-5144
  www.wga.org

APPENDIX C

Internet Resources
for Screenwriters

Contributed by Debra Stone

Absolute Write
    www.absolutewrite.com
    Writing website for all genres. Good articles.

Academy of Motion Pictures
    www.oscars.org
    Website of the Academy

Actors and Their Agents
    http://modigliani.brandx.net/user/musofire/talent.csv.txt
    Database of actor/actress contacts

Ain't It Cool News
    www.aint-it-cool-news.com
    Gossip and info on upcoming movies and projects

American Film Institute
    www.afionline.com
    Film organization website

American Zoetrope (AZ)
    www.zoetrope.com
    Online peer review. Terrific resource for feedback/workshopping your scripts

Ask Dr. Hollywood
    http://home.earthlink.net/%7Edare2b/faq.htm
    Question and answers from an industry pro

Atom Films
    www.atomfilms.com
    Site for shorts

Celluloid Jungle
    www.celluloidjungle.com
    Comprehensive screenwriting and research site

Christopher Vogler
www.thewritersjourney.com
Chris Vogler, author of *The Writer's Journey*, adapts Joseph Campbell's concepts for screenwriters

Cineparlance
http://www.netwiz.net/~rdef/cineparlance/cineparlance.htm
Interviews with directors

Creative Screenwriting
www.creativescreenwriting.com
Screenwriter magazine

Directors Guild of America
www.dga.org
Directors website

Done Deal
www.scriptsales.com
Script sales and marketing info

Drews Script-O-Rama
www.script-o-rama.com
Scripts you can download

Fade In
www.fadeinmag.com
Screenwriting magazine

Film Tracker
www.filmtracker.com
Site with various industry folk networking

Film.com
http://www.film.com/watch/interviews.html
Interviews and streaming video

Filmmaker
www.filmmakers.com
Site about making films

Goodstory
www.goodstory.com
Pay site to upload scripts—agents are referring queries here

Hollywood Book City
http://www.hollywoodbookcity.com/cgi-bin/mvscript.cgi
Order scripts online ($$)

Hollywood Creative Directory
www.hcdonline.com
Production company and agent/manager directory ($$)

Hollywood Lit Sales
www.hollywoodlitsales.com
Upload loglines; also a great site (cheap) for script sales

Hollywood Movie News
www.hollywood.com
Movie news and gossip

Hollywood Net
www.hollywoodnet.com
Associated with the Hollywood Film Festival

Hollywood Network
http://actors.com/Buzzell/board
Screenwriting information and contact source

Hollywood Reporter
www.hollywoodreporter.com
Movie and industry news and articles (free and $$)

IMDb
www.imdb.com
Movie database—very comprehensive

In Hollywood
www.inhollywood.com
"Who's Who" directory, current projects, e-mails ($$)

Inside
www.inside.com
Online trade magazine

International Entertainment
www.medialawyer.com
Ask free entertainment questions, and articles

InZide
www.inzide.com
Screenwriting information and logline submission

JoBlo's Movie Scripts
http://www.joblo.com/moviescripts.htm
Free online script download

Linda Seger
www.lindaseger.com
Script consulting services and seminars

Movie Bytes
www.moviebytes.com
Screenwriting contests and who's buying what (free and $$)

Movie Screenplay Links
http://www.kolumbus.fi/rukkila/scripts.htm
Free online script download

New York Screenwriter
www.nyscreenwriter.com
Screenwriting website

Point of View Magazine
www.empire-pov.com
Articles and interviews with industry professionals

Producer Link
www.producerlink.com
Producer credits, contact info, box office (free and $$)

Screenplay 451
http://www.pumpkinsoft.de/screenplay451/alpha1.htm
Free online script download

Screenplayers
www.screenplayer.net
Group of writers with good articles

Screenwriters Online
www.screenwriter.com
Online classes ($$)

Screenwriters Utopia
www.screenwritersutopia.com
Screenwriting website

Script Online Ezine
www.scriptmag.com/ezine_plus/
eZine

Script Shack
www.scriptshack.com
Order scripts online ($$)

Scripterz
http://chat.scripterz.org/
Online script critique group

Show Biz Data
www.showbizdata.com
Database of contacts, credits, and projects ($$)

Simply Scripts
http://simplyscripts.home.att.net/
Free online script download

Syd Field Presents
www.sydfield.com/splash.htm
Syd Field's screenwriting site

The Daily Script
www.dailyscript.com
Free online script download

The Source
www.thesource.com
Script submissions and consultation (free and $$)

TV Writer
www.tvwriter.com
Devoted to television writing

Variety
www.variety.com
Movie and industry news and articles (free and $$)

Who Represents
www.whorepresents.com
Check which agent reps talent/writers

Women in Film
www.wif.org
Networking site promotes women in film

Wordplay
www.wordplayer.com
Screenwriting site by industry pros

Writers Digest
  www.writersdigest.com
  Magazine for all genres

Writers Guild of America
  www.wga.org
  Writers Guild website

APPENDIX D

Resources: Publications

These are the books (listed alphabetically by author) and periodicals I have found to be the most inspiring and helpful to me as a screenwriter.

Books

The Screenwriter's Survival Guide, by Max Adams (Warner Books, 2001)

Zen and the Art of Writing, by Ray Bradbury (Joshua Odell Editions, Santa Barbara, 1994)

The Hero With a Thousand Faces, by Joseph Campbell (Princeton University Press, 1949)

The Writing Life, by Annie Dillard (Harper Perennial, 1989)

Screenplay, by Syd Field (Dell Trade Paperback, 1979).

Wild Mind, by Natalie Goldberg (Bantam Press, 1990)

Writing Down the Bones, by Natalie Goldberg (Shambhala, 1986)

Adventures in the Screen Trade, by William Goldman (Warner Books, 1989)

On Writing: A Memoir of the Craft, by Stephen King (Scribner, 2000)

Bird by Bird, by Anne Lamott (Pantheon Books, 1994)

The First Time I Got Paid for It: Writers' Tales from the Hollywood Trenches, edited by Peter Lefcourt and Laura J. Shapiro (Public Affairs, 2000)

On the Art of Writing, by Sir Arthur Quiller-Couch, 1916 (Fowey Rare Books, 1995 ed.)

Making a Good Script Great, by Linda Seger (Samuel French, 1987).

The Writer's Journey, by Christopher Vogler (Michael Wiese Productions, 1992)

Periodicals

Creative Screenwriting

Entertainment Weekly

Premiere Magazine

Scenario

Script

The Writer

Writers Digest

Written By (Writers Guild of America)

APPENDIX E
Screenwriting Contests

For a complete list of screenplay competitions, go to moviebytes.com.

Current Favorites

A.F.I. Maui Conference
   International Screenwriting Competition
   2021 N. Western Ave.
   Los Angeles, CA 90027-1657

   Attn: Joe Petricca
   (808) 879-0061
   www.mauiwriters.com
   mauiscript@aol.com

   Deadline: July 1
   $2,500 for 1st (plus free Maui retreat); $1,000 for 2nd; $500 for 3rd place
   Eligible: Any screenplays not sold and never optioned

Austin Film Festival
   Heart of Film Screenplay Competition
   1604 Nueces
   Austin, TX 78701

   (512) 478-4795
   (512) 478-6205 (fax)
   www.austinfilmfestival.com

   Deadline May 15
   $5,000 prize, plus trip to Austin
   Entry fee: $40
   Eligible: All writers who do not make their living writing film or TV

Chesterfield Film Co.
  Writers Film Project
  1158 26th Street, Box 544
  Santa Monica, CA 90403

  (213) 683-3977
  www.chesterfield-co.com
  info@chesterfield-co.com

  Deadline: May 15
  $20,000 fellowship
  Entry fee: $39.50
  Eligible: Open to all.

Moondance International Film Festival
  970 Ninth Street
  Boulder, CO 80302

  (303) 545-0202
  www.moondancefilmfestival.com
  moondanceff@aol.com

  Deadline: October 15
  Entry fee: $25 to $75
  Several awards in different categories
  Check website for details
  Eligible: Anyone

Nicholl Fellowship
  Academy Foundation
  8949 Wilshire Blvd.
  Beverly Hills, CA 90211-1972

  (310) 247-3059
  www.oscars.org/nicholl/index.html

  Deadline: May 1.
  Up to $30,000 fellowships.
  Entry fee: $30
  Eligible: Any screenwriter who has not earned more than $5,000 for
    screenwriting

Scriptapalooza
    7775 Sunset Blvd., PMB #200
    Hollywood, CA 90046

    (323) 654-5809
    (323) 650-5824 (fax)
    www.scriptapalooza.com
    info@scriptapalooza.com

    Deadline: April 30
    $25,000 for 1st place; $3,000 for 2nd; $2,000 for 3rd place
    Entry fee: $40 to $50 (depending on whether early or late)
    Eligible: Anyone

Sundance Institute
    8857 W. Olympic Blvd.
    Beverly Hills, CA 90211

    (310) 394-4662
    (310) 394-88353 (fax)
    www.sundance.org

    Deadline: May 4
    Prize: Participation at Sundance residential lab, and travel expenses
    Entry fee: $30
    Eligible: Must live in U.S.

APPENDIX F
Agencies

CAA
Creative Artists Agency
9830 Wilshire Blvd.
Beverly Hills, CA 90212
(310) 288-4545
(310) 288-4800 (fax)

ICM
International Creative Management
8942 Wilshire Blvd.
Beverly Hills, CA 90211
(310) 550-4000
(310) 550-4100 (fax)

UTA
United Talent Agency
9560 Wilshire Blvd., 5th Floor
Beverly Hills, CA 90212
(310) 273-6700
(310) 247-1111 (fax)

William Morris Agency
151 El Camino Drive
Beverly Hills, CA 90212
(310) 859-4000
(310) 859-4419 (fax)

For a complete list of screenwriters' agents, contact the Agency Department of the Writers Guild of America, at (323) 782-4502 or online at www.wga.org.

APPENDIX G

Author's Background

Books & Other Nonfiction

The Writer's Guide to Writing Your Screenplay (The Writer Books, 2002).

Screenwriting columnist, *Writer's Digest*, 1998-2001.

Monthly writing column, *The Willamette Writer*, 1995 to present.

Television Miniseries

Buffalo Girls. Writer. CBS miniseries (four hours). From the novel by Larry McMurtry. Produced by Suzanne de Passe. Starring Anjelica Huston, Melanie Griffith, Reba McEntire, Gabriel Byrne, Sam Elliott, Jack Palance, and Peter Coyote. Aired April 30 and May 1, 1995. Nominated for eleven Emmy Awards including Best Miniseries.

I Know My First Name Is Steven. Co-writer. NBC miniseries (four hours). Aired May 22 and 23, 1989. Emmy nomination: Best Miniseries, Best Teleplay.

Degree of Guilt. Writer/co-producer. NBC miniseries (four hours). From the novels by Richard North Patterson. Aired October 29 and 30, 1995.

Felicity, Kirsten, Samantha, Molly, Addy, Josefina. Screenwriter. Six four-hour miniseries. From the books published by American Girls. Pleasant Company. 1993 to 2000.

Sinatra. (Uncredited.) Worked with Tina Sinatra and Mr. Sinatra for seven months. Revised William Mastrosimone's eight-hour script to five-hour shooting script. Winner of Emmy for Best Miniseries.

Movies of the Week (TV)

The View From Saturday. Based on the 2000 Newberry Award-winning children's book by E. L. Konigsberg. Showtime/Nickelodeon, in development.

Selma, Lord, Selma. ABC Movie of the Week. Aired Martin Luther King Jr. Day, January 17, 1999. Based on the book by Sheyann Webb and Rachel West Nelson. Introduced by Coretta Scott King. Nominated for NAACP *Image* Award.

Best Friends For Life. Writer. CBS Movie of the Week. Aired January 18, 1998. Starring Gena Rowlands, Linda Lavin, and Richard Farnsworth. Based on the novel *Life Estates* by Shelby Hearon.

Emma's Wish. CBS Movie of the Week. Writer/Producer. Aired October 1998. Starring Joanna Kerns and Della Reese.

The Search for Grace. Executive Producer. CBS Movie of the Week. Starring Lisa Hartman Black and Ken Wahl. Aired May 17, 1994.

Mark Twain and Me. Writer. Disney Channel. December 1991. Starring Jason Robards as Mark Twain. Directed by Dan Petrie, Sr. Winner, Emmy Award and Cable Ace Award for Best Children's Program.

Guilty . . . Until Proven Innocent. NBC Movie of the Week. Fall 1991. Writer and co-producer. Starring Martin Sheen and Brendan Fraser.

When You Remember Me. ABC Movie of the Week. Co-writer. Aired October 7, 1990. Starring Fred Savage, Kevin Spacey, and Ellen Burstyn.

Follow Your Heart. NBC Movie of the Week. Co-writer. Aired April, 1990. Starring Patrick Cassidy and Frances Sternhagen.

Body of Evidence. CBS Movie of the Week. Writer. Aired January 1988. Produced and directed by Roy Campanella, II. Starring Barry Bostwick and Margot Kidder.

One Terrific Guy. CBS Movie of the Week. Writer. Aired February 1986. Starring Wayne Rogers and Marriette Hartley.

Grace Kelly. ABC Movie of the Week. Writer. February 1983. Starring Cheryl Ladd.

Jane Doe. CBS Movie of the Week. Co-writer. March 1983. Starring Karen Valentine, William Devane, Eva Marie Saint.

Eleanor, First Lady of the World. CBS Movie of the Week. Co-writer. May 1982. Starring Jean Stapleton as Eleanor Roosevelt.

Not in Front of the Children. CBS Movie of the Week. October 1982. Writer. Starring Linda Gray and John Lithgow.

Leave 'Em Laughing. CBS Movie of the Week. Starring Mickey Rooney, Red Buttons, and Anne Jackson. Directed by Jackie Cooper.

Feature Film Scripts

e-tickets. Original screenplay in development by Producer Alex Rose

(Author has sold/developed a total of 14 scripts at major studios that have not been filmed.)

Plays

Look Away. KCET Public Television. Adapted from the play by Jerome Kilty. November 1987. Starring Ellen Burstyn as Mary Todd Lincoln.

Looking Glass. Co-written with Michael Sutton. Produced Off-Broadway, 1982, at Entermedia Theatre, New York. A play about Lewis Carroll. Published by Broadway Plays.

Awards and Honors

Oregon Film Office Board—Oregon Literary Arts Advisory Board.

Humanitas Award, Nominee, *Selma, Lord, Selma*, 1999.

Paul Selvin Award, Writers Guild of America, *Guilty Until Proven Innocent*.

Writers Guild Award Nominee, *Guilty Until Proven Innocent*, 1993.

Cable Ace Award Nominee, *Mark Twain and Me*, 1993.

Humanitas Award Nominee, *Mark Twain and Me*, 1993.

Silver Nymph Award, Monaco International Television Festival, *Guilty Until Proven Innocent*, 1993.

Christopher Award, Catholic Church, *When You Remember Me*, 1991.

Emmy Award Nominee, *I Know My First Name Is Steven*, 1989.

Writers Guild Award Nominee, *I Know My First Name Is Steven*, 1990.

Emmy Award Nominee (L.A. Area), *Look Away*, 1988.

Edgar Allan Poe Award Nominee, *Jane Doe*, 1983.

Humanitas Award Nominee, *Leave 'Em Laughing*, 1981.

Samuel Goldwyn Writing Award, 1973.

Graduated Magna Cum Laude from UCLA Film School.

Teaching

UCLA Film School, Advanced Screenwriting. 1984 through 1991.

Advanced Screenwriting, Portland, Oregon

Available in Video

Of the author's films, three are currently available for rental in video:

Buffalo Girls

Mark Twain and Me

Selma, Lord, Selma

Answers to the Most Common Questions

As you approach the jumping-off place, from writing your screenplay in private to plunging into the Hollywood marketplace, here are some of the answers to new screenwriters' most-asked questions.

1 Do you have to live in L.A.? No. In our increasingly placeless society, the physical location of a writer is becoming less and less important. You will have to go to L.A. for some meetings, but once you are hired, they will usually fly you in. Many meetings now happen by conference calls. And scripts can be delivered instantly by e-mail or overnight by FedEx.

2 Do you have to have an agent first? No. Get anyone in the business you can to read your script. I recommend you send it to agents and producers, actors with production deals, and directors who also produce. Once you have interest, it's easier to get an agent. You don't know where the crack in the wall is going to show up, so keep firing at it from every direction until you find an opening.

3 What is a "release form" and should I sign one? "Release forms" are standard procedure, and most producers and studios require that you sign one before they read your script if you don't have an agent. The fine print may be alarming, but you are basically promising you won't sue them if they have a similar project in development.

4 What is an option? It is a contract giving a producer a specified amount of time to try and sell your script. The amount of money ranges from nominal ($1) to phenomenal (for a bestselling book, for example). Options are usually for six months to a year, plus renewal clauses. If you believe in that producer's ability to set projects up, go for it. On the other hand, a studio may pass on your project if the producer isn't someone they like—and once it has been all over town, even the shiniest new script gets shopworn.

5 Is a Writers Guild strike a great opportunity for new writers to break in? No. Once the stores are closed, the serious shoppers tend to stop looking. Hollywood pretty much shuts down during major strikes. And if you do sell a script during a strike, the Writers Guild will not look kindly on it when you come in later, ready to join.

6 I know of a true story that would make a great movie. Do I have to get the rights? Yes. People own their own life stories, unless they are celebrities. You can do an unauthorized biography of Napoleon or Madonna, but your Uncle Benny could sue you for writing the story of his escape from Alcatraz, and he'd win. However, most people are happy to have their stories told. Ask Uncle Benny, and write up a simple letter of agreement in which he gives you permission to tell his story—and says that if it sells, he will be paid "fair market value" for the rights. The specific amount can be negotiated later. If you love the story and can't get the rights, you can do a fictional version, but it has to be different in most major aspects: characters, setting, sequence of events, etc. In other words, if in your script, Benny is now a female prisoner escaping from an insane asylum in 1852, you'll be fine.

7 Someone came to me with a story idea. They want me to write the screenplay and if it sells, we'll split the money. Should I do this? Only if it's a once-in-a-lifetime fabulous idea. Collaboration is often twice the work for half the fee. Or in this case, you'd be doing all the work for half the money. And a screenplay that isn't an original story and script by one person is often not considered suitable as a writing sample to get you other assignments. I recommend this if only you have no good ideas of your own to write.

8 Someone likes my script but wants me to rewrite it for free. I don't have a contract. Should I do it? On two conditions only: 1) The changes they are suggesting make it a much better script. And 2) If everyone is clear that even if you make the changes they suggest, this in no way gives them any degree of ownership of the script. If they want that, they will have to buy or option the script, sign a contract with you, and pay you. Producers often feel that if they have "worked on a script" with a writer, it is "their script." This is *not* the case. Until someone else buys your writing, it belongs wholly and solely to you.

[cont.]

9 Can a writer have creative control? No. This is a fantasy. It doesn't exist. It is easier to get to direct your own movie than to be granted "creative control." Directors don't even have final cut, for the most part. If you are personable and easy to work with, you may be welcome at read-throughs, on the set, and in dailies. The filmmakers may not ask your opinion, but you are free to give it to them anyway. Sometimes they even listen.

10 I've written a book (or article) that would make a good Hollywood movie. Do I have to write the screenplay in order to sell it to Hollywood? No. They are in the market for "projects," and those often come in the form of books, stories, or articles. *Proof of Life*, for example, is a major motion picture based on a magazine story. If you have a literary agent, ask him to submit your book or story to the Hollywood marketplace. Or you can send query letters to agents and producers, just as you would for a screenplay.

11 Do I have to be a member of the Writers Guild of America to sell a script? No. You are free to sell scripts to any of the movie markets. But to be hired to rewrite a script or for a development deal by a company that is signatory to WGA (i.e., all the major entertainment companies), you must join. And you must have sold at least one script to be eligible to join. The benefits in terms of medical coverage, pension, and residuals alone are well worth the fees and dues.

12 Should I read the trades? "The trades" are what Hollywood calls the two major daily newspaper, *Variety* and *The Hollywood Reporter*. However, I don't recommend this. The amount of information they contain is far beyond what is useful or beneficial to an aspiring writer. Instead, if you want to keep a finger on the pulse of Hollywood, read a more general movie periodical like *Entertainment Weekly*, or *Premiere* magazine. Read the entertainment section of your local newspapers. Read the reviews, go to the movies, and track box-office scores. Before you compare your new script to a major movie, know whether it was considered a box-office disappointment. Even movies grossing $100 million can be bombs—if they cost $120 million to make.

The more you understand about the entertainment industry, the easier the transition will be from sandlot dreamer to rookie slugger in the major leagues. When your script is ready, don't hesitate to step up to the plate.

Acknowledgments

Doris S. Michaels, my book agent, for finding me, and for understanding this book immediately and placing it perfectly.

Dave Wirtschafter, my screenwriting agent.

Laurie Pozmantier, my television agent.

Tony Bill, who gave me my first screenwriting job.

My family for a lifetime of support. My parents, David and Susanne Whitcomb. My sisters, Wendy Marsh and Laura Whitcomb, and my brother, Jonathan Whitcomb.

Sat-Kaur for loving friendship and daily support, saving me untold fortunes in therapy bills, and helping me maintain spiritual clarity in the midst of the fray.

Hilary Leach for thirty years of Best Friendship. Between us we can always find something to laugh about, even in the darkest hours.

Laura Whitcomb, delightful company, lifelong support, and love, and an inspiration, always.

Ruth Maxwell, a role model and a dear, dear friend.

My Women's Writing Support Group: Leona Grieve, Linda Leslie, Kristi Negri, Cherie Walter, Jackie Blain, and Laura Whitcomb. Without our writing marathons at Cannon Beach, this book would not have been finished this year.

My weekly writing support partner, Rachel Hardesty.

My assistant Kirsten Kill for helping manage the details of life so I could get the writing done. And Preston, our beloved mascot.

Writers Digest for giving me a forum to develop some of this material as their Scripts Columnist. My editors there over the years, especially Katie Dumont.

Willamette Writers and its board members for giving me a writing home and family in the Pacific Northwest. The W.W. newsletter that has been a safe place to develop as a nonfiction writer. Our brilliant editor Leona Grieve.

Debra Stone for generously contributing the Internet Guide included in the appendices, and for being a remarkable person and friend.

My colleagues Mike Rich, Max Adams, Julian Fowles, Linda Seger, Alex Rose, Christopher Vogler, and especially Michael Colleary, Mike Werb, and Neil Landau, of whom I am very proud.

My students at UCLA and in Portland, Oregon, who have taught me so much in the process of my teaching them.

My Book Club for keeping me reading and thinking.

My dear friends Laurie Draper, Peggy Walton-Walker, Carol Marmaduke, Gail Neuberg, Pamela Smith Hill, Susan Fletcher, Debbie Stone, Elizabeth Neeld, Denise Koch, Jane Alden, Sharron Pettengill, Paul Duchene, Mark Wigginton, Barbara Lindsay, Bill Johnson, Jackie Blain, Philece Sampler, Linda Hampton, Mark Vahanian, John Vickery, Henry Marsh, and David H. Bell.

My stepson, Jake. An inspiration and a great kid.

Sam, wherever you are, we love you.

My children Nick and Molly. You are my home, my family, and my joy. The top of my list of what makes life worth living. Thank you.

Index

The Writer

The Writer was founded in 1887 by two reporters from the *Boston Globe*. Their mission was to publish a magazine that would be "helpful, interesting, and instructive to all literary workers." The magazine soon became an essential resource for writers, publishing articles in the first half of the 20th century by literary luminaries such as William Carlos Williams, Wallace Stegner, Sinclair Lewis, William Saroyan, Daphne du Maurier, and many others.

After a long editorial tenure into the latter half of the 20th century by A. S. Burack and then Sylvia K. Burack, Kalmbach Publishing Co. purchased the magazine in the year 2000, along with its affiliated line of books on writing fiction and nonfiction, and moved the editorial operations from Boston to Waukesha, Wisconsin, a suburb of Milwaukee.

Continuing its long heritage of more than 110 years of service, now into the 21st century, *The Writer* magazine continues to be an essential resource for writers, providing advice from our most prominent writers, featuring informative articles about the art and the business of writing.

It is dedicated to helping and inspiring writers to succeed in their endeavors and to fostering a sense of community among writers everywhere.

More information on *The Writer*, with current articles and other resources, can be found online at http://www.writermag.com.

—Elfrieda Abbe, Editor
The Writer